A SAINSBURY COOKBOOK

VEGETARIAN
—MEALS—

ROSAMOND
RICHARDSON

CONTENTS

Published exclusively for J Sainsbury plc
Stamford House Stamford Street
London SE1 9LL
by Martin Books
Simon & Schuster International Group
Fitzwilliam House 32 Trumpington Street
Cambridge CB2 1QY

ISBN 0 85941 542 2

First published 1984
New enlarged edition 1985
Eighth impression 1989

Text and photographs © J Sainsbury plc 1984, 1989

Printed in Great Britain

THE AUTHOR

Rosamond Richardson is the author of several books, and presenter of BBC TV's 'Discovering Patchwork' and co-presenter of BBC TV's 'Discovering Hedgerows'. She has also done a short cookery series for BBC East and a series on the uses of herbs for Anglia Television. She has been a regular contributor to BBC Radio Cambridgeshire. As well as publications to accompany her television series, her books include *Hedgerow Cookery, Cooking for Kids, The Little Garlic Book, The Little Mushroom Book, The Little Nut Book* and *Memorable Meals in Minutes*.

Rosamond lives in a small Essex village with her husband and three children.

INTRODUCTION

There is an enormous range of dishes that you can make without including meat, dishes that make appetising and delicious meals catering for all seasons and all tastes. You do not have to be a vegetarian to enjoy the marvellous food you can cook without using meat or fish. Awaiting you is a catalogue of mouth-watering ingredients which you can serve in a myriad of ways: mushrooms, cheese, pasta, rice, crêpes, vol-au-vents, quiches, eggs, pulses, nuts, olives, fresh herbs and garlic. Meat is much the same the world over, which cannot be said of the extraordinary range of vegetables and fruit grown in different climates and nations. Just think what a restricted range of foods was available to our forefathers: we are incredibly lucky to live in an age where distance is no object and fresh produce can be shipped from far and wide at very reasonable cost. We are spoiled for choice!

With such a range to choose from I could personally live perfectly happily on meatless meals (in fact I do) without feeling in the least deprived. I have discovered novel combinations of taste and texture using all these good things, cooking them in good olive oil or butter, and trying out new mixtures of herbs and spices to highlight them. Whilst I was testing the recipes for this book I discovered that children were just as happy – if not happier – with a meatless menu, because it is all so tasty and smells so good! As for my contemporaries and elders, I don't think they even noticed that the meals *were* meatless, so appetising and nourishing were they, and often alluringly prettier than many meat dishes.

Apart from manifestly enjoying this type of food, you will find that it has all kinds of other advantages. A well balanced, meatless diet can be very good for your health, as it is nutritious, low in fats and high in bulk and fibre. Many of the healthiest countries in the world live on meatless meals, and so we can rest assured that

Note on quantities

Ingredients in the recipes are given in both imperial (oz, fl oz, etc) and metric (g, ml, etc) measures. Use either set of quantities, but not a mixture of both, in any one recipe. All spoon measures are level spoons unless otherwise stated (metric spoon measures are always level). Egg size, where not specified, is medium (size 3).

we are giving our bodies the optimum chance of retaining good health. Some of the recipes in this book suit vegan diets, and even some special or diabetic regimes. For those who are weight conscious, and for those who are slimming, eating meatless meals can be an easy way to keep your figure looking good: you can eat vegetables in quantity, if in the proper balance, without any risk to your health. The variety and tastiness of a slimming regime based on pulses, vegetables, salads and fruit make it a very pleasant one – a far cry from deprivation! Low in calories, high in bulk and fibre, it is so delicious and satisfying that you will hardly notice that you are on a diet!

Meals without meat are also significantly cheaper than their counterparts – no mean consideration. You can eat as well, if not better, for far less than when consuming traditional Western cooking. They also have the advantage that you can organise things so that in times of glut, during the summer months particularly, you can ensure no waste. Many of the recipes in this book freeze extremely well, so cash in on a time of plenty, buy up whatever produce is really cheap and you will be able to pull all sorts of goodies out of the freezer through the leaner months of winter. With a little bit of rethinking and a few changes of habit, you will find that you are eating nutritious and delicious meals all the year round, for far less than you would ever have dreamed.

Apart from all these positive advantages, meatless meals simply make a nice change from the usual pattern of eating: they are refreshingly different. Just for fun, try converting a confirmed carnivore – it worked for me. Not only was the principal guinea-pig for this book (one carnivorous husband) appreciative of the dishes, he was also appreciative of how kind they were to the housekeeping budget!

The thing about using all the ingredients in this book is that they lend themselves to a whole spectrum of styles – from the plainest of home cooking to the most elegant of entertaining dishes; from the blandest of flavours to the spiciest and most exotic tastes. Some of the concoctions you can make are really epicurean, and I have produced many a little party dish which has been enthusiastically acclaimed, and the recipe demanded of me. People generally seem to like something different, original and light for a dinner party, and there are endless combinations that you can try out without using meat, to achieve truly memorable meals. From feeding the youngest of children to serving the most elegant of dinners, meals without meat have never let me down.

Basic recipes

PASTRY

4 oz (125 g) butter or vegetable margarine

6 oz (175 g) plain flour

4 tablespoons (4 × 15 ml spoon) cold water

salt

This pastry recipe is suitable for all the dishes in this book and makes two 8-inch (20 cm) pastry shells. The quantities may be varied according to the needs of each recipe, so long as the proportions of the ingredients are maintained.

Rub the fat into the flour and add a pinch of salt. Mix in the water and work to a smooth dough. Alternatively you can put all the ingredients in a blender and whizz them until the pastry has formed a ball. Chill for at least 2 hours before rolling out.

ALTERNATIVE OIL PASTRY RECIPE

12 oz (350 g) plain flour

1 teaspoon (5 ml spoon) salt

¼ pint (150 ml) vegetable oil

3 tablespoons (3 × 15 ml spoon) water

For those who prefer this method of making pastry.

Sift the flour with the salt and stir in the oil and water. Mix well and knead briefly until smooth. Do not chill or roll out but just press into a greased container with your knuckles and bake blind for 20 minutes.

BÉCHAMEL SAUCE

1½ oz (40 g) butter

2 tablespoons (2 × 15 ml spoon) plain flour

½ pint (300 ml) milk, heated

salt and pepper

A well-known white sauce which makes a creamy base for many delicious vegetarian recipes. You can vary the quantity to suit any recipe, keeping the proportions the same.

Melt the butter in a heavy saucepan. Gradually stir in the flour with a wooden spoon, and then add the milk slowly, stirring all the time until the sauce thickens. Season to taste and simmer over a very low heat for 5 minutes.

Strict vegetarians can make béchamel using vegetable margarine instead of butter, and hot vegetable stock instead of milk, in the same quantities and by the same method.

Alternatives for strict vegetarians

Stock: to make vegetable stock, take whatever vegetables are available, for example, onions, carrots, leeks, soaked lentils and jerusalem artichokes, and cover them with water in a large saucepan. Add salt, peppercorns, bay leaves and either fresh or dried herbs according to the season and bring to the boil. Simmer for 1 hour and then leave to stand till cool. Strain off and keep chilled or frozen.

Gelatine: a substitute such as agar-agar, which is available from specialist food shops, may be used in recipes which call for gelatine-based products such as Little Tomato Pies (page 10).

Puff pastry: a chilled puff pastry which does not contain animal fats is available from most branches of Sainsbury's.

Cheese: a vegetarian Cheddar cheese is available from most branches of Sainsbury's.

Cream: a non-dairy cream made with refined vegetable oil is available from most branches of Sainsbury's.

APPETISERS, HORS D'OEUVRES AND SOUPS

CHEESE WAFERS

Makes 30

4 oz (100 g) Cheddar cheese, grated

4 oz (100 g) butter, softened

3 oz (75 g) plain flour, sifted

salt and pepper and cayenne pepper to taste

Oven temperature:
Gas Mark 7/425°F/220°C

These never fail to produce a gasp of appreciation and an immediate demand for the recipe: so here it is!

Mix all the ingredients together until well blended. Place grape-sized little balls of the mixture on a greased baking sheet and flatten them down. Bake for 10–15 minutes until golden.

MUNG CRUNCH

This is a fabulous stand-by for 'nibbles'. These little crispy seeds are very tasty and it's hard to stop eating them! They are easy and cheap to make, and certainly an original change from more conventional snacks to go with drinks before a meal.

Just soak as many mung beans as you want to use, overnight. Drain them and dry thoroughly. Fry in vegetable oil over a moderate heat, turning frequently, until they are browned and crisp – between 5 and 10 minutes. Drain on kitchen paper towelling, sprinkle with salt, and cool. They store very successfully in airtight jars.

Mung Crunch
Cheese Wafers
Little Tomato Pies

LITTLE TOMATO PIES

Serves 6

Basic recipe: Pastry (page 6)

18 × 3-inch (8cm) pastry
shells made with 6 oz
(175 g) flour

For the filling:

1 packet of orange or lemon
jelly

8 oz (226 g) can of tomatoes

2 tablespoons (2 × 15 ml
spoon) chopped parsley

garlic, to taste

salt to taste

Oven temperature:
Gas Mark 4/350°F/180°C

*This recipe is a personal favourite of mine: the
miniature pies combine the sweetness of jelly, the
texture of tomatoes and a tang of herbs.*

Cook the shells for 20 minutes.
    Make the jelly as instructed on the packet and
allow to cool a little. Drain the tomatoes
thoroughly, chop them and mix them in. Add
the parsley, garlic and salt, and spoon into the
cooled pastry shells to set.

OLIVADE

Serves 6

10 oz (275 g) black olives

3 tablespoons (3 × 15 ml
spoon) olive oil

8 oz (225 g) cottage cheese,
sieved

black pepper

brandy (optional)

*To me this is a kind of inexpensive air-ticket to
Provence. Its distinctive taste recalls instantly the
landscape and shimmering heat of the South of France.
Serve with bread-sticks and Melba toast (see page
11).*

Stone the olives and liquidise them with the oil.
Mix into the sieved cottage cheese and mash to a
paste. Season with black pepper and a little
brandy if desired.

CHOU À LA CRÈME

Serves 4

1 small white cabbage,
shredded

4 oz (100 g) butter

½ pint (300 ml) double
cream

lots of black pepper

*This is a beautiful hors d'oeuvre, and the best way that
I know of eating cabbage: the cream and the black
pepper take the most ordinary of vegetables into the
realm of the epicurean.*

Blanch the shredded cabbage in boiling water,
and cool. Melt the butter and add the shredded
cabbage, and cook very slowly until it is tender.
Season liberally with black pepper, and just
before serving add the cream and heat through
thoroughly. Serve with croûtons of fried bread.

AUBERGINE PURÉE

Serves 6

2 aubergines

4–5 tablespoons (4–5 × 15
ml spoon) olive oil

3 tablespoons (3 × 15 ml
spoon) chopped parsley

2 cloves of garlic, crushed

juice of 1 lemon

salt and pepper

*This sensuous dip, with its resonances of the
Mediterranean, makes a delicious nibble to go with
drinks before a meal. Try it with crisps, or with little
squares of Melba toast (see Note below). Cheese
Wafers (page 8) go well with it, too.*

Char or bake the aubergines until they are soft
right through, about 15–20 minutes. Leave
them to cool. Peel and chop them, letting the
inside juices strain away. Blend the flesh in the
liquidiser. Add the oil gradually, stirring all the
time, and then mix in the other ingredients.
Season to taste.

Note on Melba toast: to make Melba toast, slice
white bread thinly and cut off the crusts. Place
the slices flat on a baking tray and dry out in a
very low oven, Gas Mark 2/300°F/150°C, for
1½–2 hours until crisp and golden. Cool on a
rack.

OEUFS EN GELÉE

Serves 4

4 large eggs (size 1)

4 thin slices of cucumber, peeled

10 oz (275 g) can of condensed consommé

4 tablespoons (4 × 15 ml spoon) mayonnaise

salt and pepper

To garnish:

fresh parsley, thyme and tarragon, chopped finely

The inspiration for these soft-boiled eggs covered in beautifully flavoured aspic comes from a charcuterie which I discovered on holiday in Normandy. The eggs are placed on slices of peeled cucumber and decorated with home-made mayonnaise and fresh herbs. They are mouth-watering.

Boil the eggs for 4 minutes and crack the egg shells gently before plunging them in cold water to cool. Place the cucumber slices on the bottom of ramekin dishes. Heat the consommé gently and season to taste. Peel the eggs carefully and put them in the dishes – a little consommé helps set the egg in position – cover with the consommé and chill until it jellies again. Chill the mayonnaise well. Pipe the mayonnaise over the top, sprinkle with the finely chopped herbs and serve in the dishes with fresh Granary bread.

LEEKS À LA GRECQUE

Serves 4

juice of 2 lemons

4 tablespoons (4 × 15 ml spoon) olive oil

1 pint (600 ml) water

10 peppercorns

10 coriander seeds

1 bay leaf

6 celery leaves

8 medium-size leeks

salt

To garnish:

chopped hard boiled egg

black olives

A classic vegetable starter using the prince of spices, one which is so characteristic of the taste and smell of Greek cookery – coriander seeds.

Put the lemon juice and oil with the water into a saucepan and add the herbs, spices and seasonings. Bring to the boil and simmer for 10 minutes. Put in the trimmed and washed leeks, cover and cook gently until they are tender. Allow to cool in the liquid. Lift out on to a plate and then reduce the liquid by boiling it fast. Pour over the leeks when it is cool and serve chilled, garnished with black olives and chopped egg.

Leeks à la Grecque
Oeufs en Gelée

ASPARAGUS SQUARES

Serves 4

Basic recipe: Béchamel Sauce (page 7)

*10 oz (275 g) can of
asparagus or 8 oz (225 g)
fresh asparagus*

*¼ pint (150 ml) béchamel
sauce*

a little double cream

4 small slices of bread

oil

parmesan cheese, grated

salt and pepper

Oven temperature:
Gas Mark 5/375°F/190°C

Canned asparagus is unfortunately nothing like as wonderful as its fresh counterpart, but this recipe brings out the very best of either and makes a delicious start to a meal.

Drain the asparagus, cut into 1-inch (2 cm) lengths and mix into the warm béchamel. Thin out with a little cream and season to taste. Cut the crusts off the bread and fry in oil until crisp and golden on both sides. Pile the creamed asparagus on to the fried bread, sprinkle with parmesan and bake for 10 minutes.

EGGS WITH MUSHROOM SAUCE

Serves 2

Basic recipe: Pastry (page 6); Béchamel Sauce (page 7)

*½ pint (300 ml) béchamel
sauce*

For the filling:

4 oz (100 g) mushrooms

1 oz (25 g) butter

a little double cream

2 large eggs (size 1)

*2 × 3-inch (8 cm)
individual pastry cases,
cooked and warmed*

salt and pepper

In this recipe, poached eggs in light pastry cases are covered with a delicate mushroom sauce. It makes an elegant dish, either as a starter or as a light meal if served with broccoli and fresh bread.

First, make the béchamel. Season to taste and simmer over a very low heat for 5 minutes.
Chop the mushrooms and cook in the butter until soft, about 5 minutes. Add to the béchamel and stir over a gentle heat until the flavours are well blended. Liquidise and thin out with a little cream. Season to taste. Poach the eggs and slip into the warmed pastry cases. Cover with the hot sauce and serve immediately.

AVOCADO AND SPINACH SOUP

Serves 4

8 oz (225 g) spinach

1 ripe avocado

1 oz (25 g) butter

¾ pint (450 ml) stock

¼ pint (150 ml) single cream or top of the milk

salt and pepper

Thick and warming, this is an ideal soup for winter – served either as a meal in itself with fresh bread, or else as a party starter. Its taste is exotic; serve it in small quantities, since a little goes a long way!

Boil the spinach until it is tender; then drain and chop it. Halve the avocado, discard the stone and scoop out the flesh. Melt the butter, toss the spinach in it and gradually stir in the mashed flesh of the avocado. Add the stock slowly, stirring all the time, and then liquidise. Season to taste if necessary, and thin out with cream or top of the milk. Reheat to serve.

THICK PEA SOUP

Serves 6

6 oz (175 g) dried split peas, covered with boiling water and left to soak overnight

2 pints (1.2 litres) stock

2 medium-size leeks

1 medium-size onion

3 celery sticks

8 oz (225 g) potatoes

3 large cabbage leaves

salt and pepper

To garnish:

4 tablespoons (4 × 15 ml spoon) finely chopped parsley

the leaves from a head of celery, chopped

This soup is for winter: it warms you right through to the tips of your toes! The dried peas and potatoes cook down to form a thick base for the soup, while the other vegetables provide wonderful flavours and textures.

Drain the peas and then simmer in 1 pint (600 ml) of the stock for 30 minutes. Meanwhile chop the leeks, slice the onion and celery, peel and slice the potatoes quite thinly and shred the cabbage leaves. Add all the vegetables to the pan with the remaining stock and simmer for a further 30 minutes. Season to taste and add the finely chopped parsley and chopped celery leaves.

PUMPKIN SOUP

Serves 4

1½ lb (675 g) pumpkin

4 oz (100 g) butter

1 bay leaf

¼ pint (150 ml) milk

5 fl oz (150 ml) carton of single cream

salt and pepper

This is one of the best soups I know. It is autumnal, rich and warming, with a glowing golden colour. Its taste is individual and distinctive, and when it is served with croûtons you will probably find that it is a meal in itself.

Cut the pumpkin flesh into small cubes. Heat the butter in a pan and toss the cubes in it with the bay leaf, salt and pepper; cook gently until they are pulpy. Liquidise with the milk. Add the cream, heat through, season to taste and serve with croûtons of fried bread.

CHUNKY COURGETTE SOUP

Serves 4

3 medium-size potatoes

2 leeks

1 pint (600 ml) stock

2 celery sticks, chopped finely

4 medium-size courgettes

2 oz (50 g) Cheddar cheese, grated

salt and pepper

I make this soup when the last of the courgettes are still around and the first old potatoes out of the ground. It is consoling food on the first chilly evenings of autumn.

Peel the potatoes and wash the leeks. Chop them and cook in the well seasoned stock with the celery until they are tender. Liquidise. Cut the courgettes in half lengthways and then cut across into chunks. Simmer in the purée until cooked through but still crisp. Stir in the cheese, and heat through until it melts. Season to taste and serve.

BROCCOLI AND CHEESE SOUP

Serves 4

2 onions

2 oz (50 g) butter

1 lb (450 g) broccoli

1 pint (600 ml) stock

3 oz (75 g) Cheddar cheese, grated

¼ pint (150 ml) single cream

salt and pepper

The delicacy of the flavours in this recipe makes it one of the finest of soups. It is easily special enough to serve up at a dinner party.

Peel and slice the onions and cook them in a saucepan over a gentle heat in the melted butter until they have softened. Trim and chop the broccoli and add to the pan, turning in the buttery juices for a minute or two. Add the stock and simmer for 20 minutes. Liquidise and strain through a sieve, pressing the broccoli through with the back of a wooden spoon. Season to taste and stir in the cheese and cream over a gentle heat until well amalgamated.

COLD CUCUMBER SOUP

Serves 4

2 medium-size cucumbers

2 onions

⅓ pint (200 ml) water

1 oz (25 g) butter

1 tablespoon (15 ml spoon) plain flour

⅓ pint (200 ml) stock

1 bay leaf

5 fl oz (150 ml) carton of single cream

dill and chives, chopped finely

grated lemon rind

salt and pepper

I never cease to marvel at how the very delicate flavour of cucumber comes into its own in this cold soup, which makes an elegant and light start to a summer meal.

Peel and slice the cucumbers and the onions, and reserve a few cucumber slices for garnish. Simmer in the water together with salt and pepper until very soft. Liquidise. Melt the butter and stir in the flour, and gradually pour in the stock, stirring until it is smooth. Add the bay leaf, and then add the cucumber purée gradually and simmer over a low heat, stirring to make it smooth. Add the cream, chopped herbs and grated lemon rind. Chill and serve garnished with the slices of peeled cucumber.

GREEN PEA CHOWDER

Serves 4

1 lb (450 g) frozen peas

1 pint (600 ml) milk

1 large onion, chopped

2 teaspoons (2 × 5 ml spoon) salt

2 bay leaves

a small bunch of mint, chopped

single cream, for thinning

A simple soup of beautiful colouring, delicate in flavour yet filling and nourishing – nothing could be better than this for lunch in the early days of winter, served piping hot and accompanied by garlic bread.

Simmer all the ingredients apart from the cream in a large pan for 15 minutes. Remove the bay leaves, liquidise and check the seasoning. Thin out with cream as necessary.

STUFFED TOMATOES WITH SPINACH AND PEAS

Serves 6

12 medium-size tomatoes

12 oz (350 g) spinach, cooked

8 oz (225 g) peas, cooked

2 oz (50 g) Cheddar cheese, grated

salt and pepper

Oven temperature:
Gas Mark 4/350°F/180°C

There is something quite extraordinarily good about the combination of spinach and peas as a purée. The fresh taste of tomatoes is a beautiful contrast, and I love to serve these as a starter with fresh Granary bread.

Cut a ½-inch (1 cm) slice off the top of each tomato and scoop out the flesh. Liquidise the cooked spinach with the peas and season to taste. Fill the tomatoes with the spinach mixture and cover the tops with grated cheese. Bake, with a little water in the bottom of the pan, for half an hour. Remove gently and serve hot or warm.

PEPPERS STUFFED WITH SWEETCORN

2 yellow peppers

12 oz (340 g) can of sweetcorn

a bunch of spring onion, chopped

3 stalks of celery, chopped finely

1 egg

butter for frying

salt and pepper

A symphony of golds and greens, this purée of sweetcorn lightly set with egg as a filling for yellow peppers makes an original and delicious starter served hot or warm on a bed of shredded lettuce.

Blanch the peppers in boiling water for 2 minutes, then drain, cut in half lengthways, and remove the seeds. Steam all the other vegetables for 20 minutes and cool a little. Liquidise with the egg, and season with salt and pepper. Heat the mixture gently in a little butter in a big frying pan until lightly set, stirring occasionally. Fill the halved peppers and serve on shredded lettuce.

VEGETABLES AS MAIN COURSES

STUFFED COURGETTES

8 medium-size courgettes
4 oz (100 g) cream cheese
2 oz (50 g) Gruyère cheese, grated
1 tablespoon (15 ml spoon) semolina
3 tablespoons (3 × 15 ml spoon) single cream
3 eggs, separated
3 tablespoons (3 × 15 ml spoon) parmesan cheese, grated
6 tablespoons (6 × 15 ml spoon) olive oil
salt, pepper and mixed herbs (fresh if available)

Oven temperature:
Gas Mark 6/400°F/200°C

This is a delightfully tasty dish, with its appetising combination of cheese, fresh herbs and the slightly crunchy courgette flesh. Serve it cold with a glass of chilled white wine and fresh Granary bread for a simple, summery lunch.

Cut the ends off the courgettes and slice them in half lengthways. Scoop out the seeds to leave them hollow. Mash the cream cheese, and add the grated Gruyère, semolina, cream, egg yolks and salt, pepper and herbs. Beat the egg whites until they are very stiff and fold into the mixture. Fill the hollowed-out courgettes. Place in a baking pan in half of the oil, and sprinkle with parmesan cheese. Sprinkle the rest of the oil over the top and bake for 20–25 minutes.

LENTIL LOAF

Serves 6

8 oz (225 g) lentils, soaked overnight

2 bay leaves

1 clove of garlic, crushed

2 teaspoons (2 × 5 ml spoon) salt

1 onion

4 oz (100 g) Cheddar cheese, grated

¼ pint (150 ml) tomato juice

2 eggs, beaten

fresh or dried mixed herbs

salt and pepper

Oven temperature:
Gas Mark 4/350°F/180°C

The principle behind this recipe is exactly the same as for a meat loaf, for which this is an excellent and tasty substitute. It is far better cold than hot, and all the flavours improve enormously after being left overnight.

Drain the soaked lentils, cover with water in a saucepan and add the bay leaves and garlic. Boil until tender, about 20–30 minutes, adding salt a few minutes before the end of the cooking. Drain.

Chop the onion and mix with the lentils and grated cheese . Add the tomato juice and the well beaten eggs, and season heavily with herbs and salt and pepper. Mix well, put in the loaf tin and bake for 1 hour. Allow to cool for 15 minutes in the tin, turn out and leave until cold.

MEATLESS SHEPHERD'S PIE

Serves 4

8 oz (225 g) lentils, soaked overnight

1 pint (600 ml) stock

1 bay leaf

2 oz (50 g) butter or vegetable margarine

2 onions, sliced

1½ oz (40 g) plain flour

1 teaspoon (5 ml spoon) mixed dried herbs

1 lb (450 g) mashed potatoes

salt and pepper

Oven temperature:
Gas Mark 4/350°F/180°C

As with the Lentil Loaf (see previous recipe), this pie is a surprisingly pleasant translation of a meat-based idea. Beautifully seasoned with herbs, it both smells and tastes scrumptious, and you won't have any leftovers!

Strain the lentils and cook them in ¾ pint (450 ml) of the stock with the bay leaf until tender, about 20–30 minutes. Drain, and season with salt. Heat the butter or margarine in a frying pan and fry the sliced onions until golden. Stir in the flour, add the rest of the stock gradually and stir until smooth. Mix in the lentils, and the herbs and season to taste. Put in the bottom of an ovenproof dish and cover with the mashed potatoes. Bake for 1 hour.

STUFFED CABBAGE

Serves 2

6 very large or 12 medium-size cabbage leaves

1 large onion

2 oz (50 g) butter

8 oz (225 g) spinach, cooked and well drained

6 oz (175 g) basmati rice, cooked

4 oz (100 g) Cheddar cheese, grated

1 teaspoon (5 ml spoon) dried herbs, or 1 tablespoon (15 ml spoon) fresh herbs

1 egg yolk

½ pint (300 ml) stock

salt and pepper

Oven temperature:
Gas Mark 4/350°F/180°C

This is a peasant dish, filling and nourishing with a robust flavour. It is satisfyingly cheap to make and none the worse for that – the combination of tastes is memorable.

Parboil the cabbage leaves for 2 minutes and cool. Meanwhile, chop the onion and soften in the butter, and then stir in the cooked spinach and rice and mix well. Stir in the grated cheese, herbs, salt and pepper, and bind with the egg yolk.

Put a heaped spoonful of the mixture in the centre of each cabbage leaf and wrap it up like a parcel. Arrange in an ovenproof dish and pour the stock over the top. Cover with foil and bake for 30 minutes.

STUFFED MUSHROOMS

Serves 2 as a main course, or 4 as a side dish

8 large, flat mushrooms

4 tablespoons (4 × 15 ml spoon) chopped parsley

2 oz (50 g) butter, plus extra for greasing

1 clove of garlic, crushed

2 oz (50 g) parmesan cheese, grated

2 oz (50 g) dry roasted peanuts, chopped

salt and pepper

Oven temperature:
Gas Mark 7/425°F/220°C

Mushrooms are a great favourite of mine, especially with garlic. If you can find really huge 'flats', serve this as a main course with a robust red wine and a crunchy salad. Smaller mushrooms make this a delicious side vegetable.

Remove the stalks from the mushrooms, chop them finely and cook with the parsley in 1 oz (25 g) of the butter for 5 minutes until well softened. Season well with garlic, salt and pepper. Put this mixture on to the gill surface of the mushrooms and place in a well-buttered baking dish. Sprinkle with the parmesan and nuts and bake, covered with dots of the remaining butter, for 10–15 minutes.

23

BAKED CABBAGE WITH NUTS AND CHEESE

Serves 2

Basic recipe: Béchamel Sauce (page 7)

1 small white cabbage

½ pint (300 ml) béchamel sauce

2 oz (50 g) salted peanuts, chopped

4 oz (100 g) Cheddar cheese, grated

nutmeg

salt and pepper

Oven temperature:
Gas Mark 7/425°F/220°C

The combination of peanuts with cheese is delicious, and this dish can either be a meal in its own right, or is very good with the Lentil Loaf on page 22.

Chop the cabbage fairly coarsely and boil it until it is cooked but still crunchy. Thin out the béchamel with a little of the cooking water and make layers in a greased baking dish of cabbage, sauce, chopped nuts and grated cheese. Season each layer with nutmeg, salt and pepper and finish with a layer of cheese. Bake for 15 minutes.

Baby Pizz

Baked Cabbage with Nuts and Cheese

Spicy Vegetable Casserole

25

SPICY VEGETABLE CASSEROLE

Pictured on the front cover   Serves 8

¼ pint (150 ml) olive oil

3 large onions, sliced

1 large aubergine, diced

4 medium-size potatoes, peeled and diced

8 oz (225 g) french beans, sliced into short pieces

2 tablespoons (2 × 15 ml spoon) garam masala

2 pints (1.2 litres) vegetable stock

2 peppers, 1 red and 1 green, de-seeded and sliced

half a medium-size cauliflower, divided into florets

4 oz (100 g) mushrooms, quartered

4 large tomatoes, quartered

2 bay leaves

chopped fresh herbs

8 oz (225 g) lentils or split peas, soaked overnight and cooked 'al dente' (with some bite left in them)

7 oz (200 g) can of sweetcorn

salt

Warming, nourishing and tasty, a dish like this is in no need of meat – it is a glorious feast in itself. There are no end of variations you can try – you can make it as simple or as extravagant as you like. In winter, brussels sprouts, broccoli, beetroot and carrot make welcome additions; in summer, courgettes, peas, spring onions and runner beans. Stir in some beansprouts at the last moment, or some thinly sliced fennel root, or even asparagus tips.

Heat the oil gently in a large casserole. Soften the onion in the oil for several minutes. Then cook the aubergine until it has absorbed plenty of oil.

First add the potatoes and french beans to the onion and aubergine mixture and stir until well warmed through. Sprinkle over the garam masala and stir in well, and then add the stock gradually and heat through. Add the peppers, cauliflower, mushrooms, tomatoes, bay leaves and herbs, and simmer gently for 10 minutes, covered with a lid. Then add the lentils or split peas and the sweetcorn and simmer for a further 5 minutes. Add salt to taste if necessary and it is ready to serve.

BABY PIZZAS

For the yeast base:

1½ oz (45 g) butter

5 oz (175 g) plain flour

1 egg

½ oz (15 g) fresh yeast, dissolved in 2 tablespoons (2 × 15 ml spoon) cold water

salt

a little warm water

For the filling:

3 onions, sliced

3 tablespoons (3 × 15 ml spoon) vegetable oil

1 aubergine, sliced, diced and salted

2 large tomatoes, skinned and chopped

a small bunch of coriander

1 tablespoon (15 ml spoon) tomato paste

1 large clove of garlic, crushed

4 oz (100 g) Cheddar cheese, grated

8 black olives, stoned and halved

salt and pepper

Oven temperature:
Gas Mark 7/425°F/220°C

Delicious hot as a simple supper dish, these are equally good cold as part of a buffet table. They look really appetising amongst a selection of salads, especially if you make them very small, and they will vanish in no time!

Rub the butter into the flour and add the salt. Put the egg into a well in the centre of the flour and add the yeast mixture. Mix with a little warm water and knead. Shape into a ball and leave to rise in a warm place for about 1 hour.

Cook the onions in the oil for about 10 minutes, covered, so that they are very soft. Then add the salted, drained aubergines and cook for a further 10 minutes, stirring from time to time. Add the skinned and chopped tomatoes and the chopped coriander. Combine the tomato paste with the garlic and add to the mixture. Season to taste and stir thoroughly.

Shape the dough into four equal balls and pat out into 5-inch (12 cm) rounds with the palms of your hands. Place on a well-greased baking tray and fill each circle with the mixture. Cover each one with grated cheese, decorate with the olives, and bake for 25–30 minutes.

VEGETABLE CURRY

1 lb (450 g) cauliflower

8 oz (225 g) frozen or fresh peas

1 lb (450 g) potatoes

2 oz (50 g) butter or vegetable margarine

3–4 teaspoons (3–4 × 5 ml spoon) garam masala

1 oz (25 g) plain flour

¾ pint (450 ml) stock

Curries with vegetables are to my mind more subtle and interesting than meat ones: they offer varied textures and flavours, enhanced in this recipe by the spicy garam masala. Serve with Dhal and Fried Rice Memsahib (pages 69 and 68).

Break the cauliflower into florets and boil for a couple of minutes with the peas. Peel the potatoes, cut them into good-sized cubes and boil for a few minutes. Melt the fat, stir in the garam masala and allow it to cook for a few minutes. Stir in the flour, and then add the cooked, drained vegetables and toss until well coated. Stir well with a wooden spoon and gradually add the stock, stirring until the sauce is smooth. Serve at once.

Vegetable Curr
Dhal (page 69
Fried Rice Memsahib (page 68

VEGETABLE SPRING ROLLS

Serves 6

12 Chinese egg-roll
wrappers, 9-inches (22 cm)
square

For the filling:

1½ lb (675 g) mixed
vegetables, such as chinese
leaves, peas, cauliflower,
courgettes, string beans,
artichoke hearts, etc., all
chopped finely

8 oz (225 g) beansprouts

4 oz (100 g) mushrooms,
sliced

5 tablespoons (5 × 15 ml
spoon) sesame oil

2 tablespoons (2 × 15 ml
spoon) soy sauce

Oven temperature:
Gas Mark 5/375°F/190°C

I love Chinese food, and it is amazing how simple much of it is to prepare. These are light and mouthwateringly delicious: golden and crisp on the outside, and full of exciting tastes inside!

Sprinkle the chopped, mixed vegetables with salt and mix in the beansprouts and mushrooms. Sauté in the oil for a minute or two, and add the soy sauce. Cool. Place about 2 heaped table-spoons (3 × 15 ml spoon) on each wrapper and roll up, tucking in the ends to make a parcel. Brush with oil and bake for 15–20 minutes until golden.

POTATOES WITH EGGS

Serves 2

4 medium-size potatoes

2 onions

2 oz (50 g) butter

2 eggs

salt and pepper

This is a wonderful supper dish for chilly winter evenings: comforting food which is easy to prepare and very economical. Serve it with fried mushrooms and a green vegetable such as spinach or broccoli.

Peel and slice both the potatoes and the onions very finely, and cook them together in a heavy frying pan over a gentle heat in the melted butter. Keep turning until they are softened but not too mushy, for about 20 minutes. Season with salt and pepper. Make a little hollow for each egg, break it in and put under a hot grill until the eggs are lightly set. Serve immediately.

CARROT SOUFFLÉ WITH GINGER

12 oz (350 g) carrots

1½ oz (40 g) butter

1 oz (25 g) flour

¼ pint (150 ml) cooking liquid from the carrots

½-inch (1 cm) piece of root ginger, peeled and grated

3 large eggs (size 1–2)

1 oz (25 g) parmesan cheese, grated

salt and pepper

Oven temperature:
Gas Mark 6/400°F/200°C

This is a supper dish with a difference, a beautiful way of using carrots which makes them appear really elegant! The advantage with this soufflé is that it holds its shape after it is cooked – so you don't have to sprint to the table as it comes out of the oven.

Boil the carrots, whole, for 25 minutes and then drain and purée them, reserving the cooking liquid. Melt the butter, stir in the flour and gradually add the warm liquid, stirring until you have a thick smooth sauce. Add the carrot purée, the grated ginger, and season to taste. Cool a little.

Beat the egg whites until stiff, and, without washing the beater, beat the yolks well and add to the carrot mixture. Fold in the whites lightly and pour into a well-greased baking dish. Cover with the grated cheese and bake for 30 minutes or until set.

STUFFED MARROW

Serves 6

1 medium to large marrow
1 large onion
8 outer lettuce leaves
4 oz (100 g) mushrooms
1 oz (25 g) butter
6 tablespoons (6 × 15 ml spoon) chopped parsley
2 oz (50 g) Cheddar cheese, grated
8 oz (225 g) cottage cheese, sieved
mixed dried herbs
salt and black pepper

Oven temperature:
Gas Mark 4/350°F/180°C

Every year, almost without fail, there is a glut of marrows in the shops – there certainly is in my garden! So I try to ring the changes with different stuffings for them. This one is a favourite with everyone.

Cut a lengthways slice off the marrow and scoop out the seeds to hollow out the insides. Sprinkle the flesh with salt and set aside to drain upside-down on absorbent paper.

Chop the onion and shred the lettuce leaves. Chop the mushrooms and cook in the butter for 3–4 minutes. Then mix all the ingredients together; season with lots of black pepper and a sprinkling of mixed, dried herbs.

Wipe the insides of the marrow dry and fill it with the stuffing. Replace the top slice as a lid and wrap securely in foil. Bake for 1¼–1½ hours.

VEGETABLE KEBABS

It is hard to believe that these kebabs can compete with traditional meat or fish ones. But they do: they are quite extraordinarily delicious, especially when served with the Herb Sauce on page 60, and Fried Rice Memsahib (page 68).

Make a selection of vegetables – for example, celery, aubergines, leeks, courgettes, peppers, onions, tomatoes, cauliflower, mushrooms (all raw). Cut into 2-inch (5 cm) lengths and marinate in olive oil and dried mixed herbs for about an hour, turning them occasionally. Skewer and grill under a medium heat for 15–20 minutes, adding later courgettes which take 10 minutes to cook, and tomatoes and mushrooms which take only 5. Turn occasionally, until they are cooked through. You are in for a delicious surprise!

Vegetable Kebabs

CORN CURRY

Serves 4

1 large onion

1-inch piece of root ginger, grated

1 large clove of garlic

2 oz (50 g) dry-roasted peanuts

a small bunch of coriander

1 teaspoon (5 ml spoon) garam masala

2 oz (50 g) butter or vegetable margarine

2 tablespoons (2 × 15 ml spoon) vegetable oil

12 oz (335 g) can of sweetcorn, drained

¼ pint (150 ml) coconut milk, made by infusing 2 oz (50 g) desiccated coconut in ¼ pint (150 ml) boiling water

2 large potatoes, boiled

oil for frying

salt

This is so simple to make, yet serve it with rice, chutney and papadoms and you have a meal fit for a maharajah.

Liquidise the onion with the ginger, garlic, nuts, coriander, garam masala and salt and cook in the fat and vegetable oil for 5 minutes over a moderate heat. Add the sweetcorn and mix well. Stir in the coconut milk and simmer for 10 minutes. Slice the potatoes and fry until golden all over, and then add to the curry.

STUFFED PEPPERS

Serves 2

1 large red pepper
2 medium-size onions
1½ oz (40 g) butter
8 oz (226 g) can of tomatoes, well drained and chopped
4 tablespoons (4 × 15 ml spoon) chopped parsley
2 oz (50 g) Cheddar cheese, grated
1 teaspoon (5 ml spoon) mixed dried herbs
1 clove of garlic, crushed
1 oz (25 g) parmesan cheese, grated
salt and pepper

Oven temperature:
Gas Mark 5/375°F/190°C

I love red peppers – their strong and exotic flavour always conjures up in my mind memories of holidays abroad, of the continental smells of garlic and good olive oil wafting from busy cafés in the hot sun.

Parboil the pepper, whole, for 3 minutes, cool quickly under cold running water and when cool halve it and take out the seeds and stalk. Peel and chop the onions and cook in the butter until soft. Add the drained, chopped tomatoes, chopped parsley and grated cheese and stir until well amalgamated. Season to taste with dried herbs and garlic, and check the seasoning for salt and pepper. Heap the mixture into the two halves of the pepper and sprinkle with the grated parmesan. Bake for 20 minutes.

VEGETABLE RISOTTO

Serves 6

6 tablespoons (6 × 15 ml spoon) vegetable oil
3 onions, sliced
2 tablespoons (2 × 15 ml spoon) garam masala
a small bunch of fresh coriander
8 oz (225 g) each of peas, beans, carrots, cauliflower
1 medium-size aubergine
4 cardamom pods
8 oz (225 g) rice, washed
salt and pepper

This is a particular favourite of mine – it is so versatile because you can use whatever vegetables are in season throughout the year, and spice it according to your taste. All it needs is a fresh green salad to go with it, and a glass or two of full red wine.

Heat the oil and fry the onions for 5 minutes. Stir in the garam masala. Add the rice and stir again. Add water to cover and simmer until cooked. Add the rest of the vegetables about 7–10 minutes before the end, so that they do not become too soft. Check the seasoning and leave until ready to serve.

FLANS, PIES, PANCAKES AND VOL-AU-VENTS

BASIC PANCAKE MIXTURE

Makes 12 pancakes

5 oz (150 g) plain flour

2 large eggs (size 1)

½ pint (300 ml) milk

¼ pint (150 ml) water

1 teaspoon (5 ml spoon) vegetable oil

a pinch of salt

Everyone has their own favourite pancake batter; this is mine. It makes thin, light pancakes which nevertheless are beautifully pliable to wrap around tasty stuffings. I make a batch of two dozen at a time and freeze them in a plastic bag, separated by little squares of foil. Either invent your own stuffings or use the three that follow to make delicious meals for everybody.

Sift the flour with the salt and make a well in the centre. Break in the eggs and mix in the flour with a wooden spoon. Gradually add the milk and water, stirring well so that it becomes completely smooth. Add the oil and leave to stand in a cool place for 3 hours.

Alternative method: put all the ingredients in the liquidiser and blend for 1 minute. Leave to stand in a cool place for 3 hours.

Cooking pancakes is just a question of practice. You need a heavy-bottomed frying pan which is just lightly greased, and which must be heated through to exactly the right temperature, but not so hot that it smokes the fat or burns the pancakes. Cook 1 tablespoonful (15 ml spoon) of the mixture at a time, spreading it over the pan. You may need to loosen the edges of the pancakes from the pan before you toss them, and allow 1 minute on each side to cook them through.

Three fillings for pancakes: Sweetcorn and Mushroom; Spinach and Onion; Ratatouille

RATATOUILLE PANCAKES

Basic recipe: Basic Pancake Mixture (page 36)

14 oz (397 g) can of tomatoes
1 small cucumber
2 onions
1 green pepper
garlic to taste
chopped fresh herbs
4 pancakes
2 oz (50 g) cheese
a little butter or oil
salt and pepper

Oven temperature:
Gas Mark 4/350°F/180°C

I have an 'instant' way of making ratatouille, which although not quite as good as the real thing is still surprisingly tasty for the small amount of effort it requires, and makes a delicious filling for pancakes. Of course, if you have the 'real thing' as a leftover, it is ideal for a pancake filling – but, if not, here is the quick method.

Drain and chop the tomatoes, peel, de-seed and dice the cucumber, finely slice the onions and cut the pepper into thin strips, discarding the seeds and the pith. Put all in a pan with crushed garlic to taste, and the chopped fresh herbs of your choice. Simmer for 10 minutes and season to taste with salt and pepper. Put 2–3 heaped tablespoons (3–4 × 15 ml spoon) of the mixture on the middle of each pancake, roll them up and put them in an ovenproof dish. Dot with butter or oil, sprinkle with the grated cheese and bake for 25 minutes.

SWEETCORN AND MUSHROOM FILLING

Serves 4

Basic recipes: Basic Pancake Mixture (page 36); Béchamel Sauce (page 7)

1½ oz (40 g) butter

12 oz (350 g) mushrooms, sliced

11 oz (335 g) can of sweetcorn

½ pint (300 ml) thick béchamel sauce

a large bunch of parsley

8 pancakes

salt and pepper

Melt the butter and cook the sliced mushrooms briefly in it until they are cooked but not too softened. Drain the sweetcorn and stir in with the mushrooms. Add this mixture to the béchamel and add the finely chopped parsley. Season to taste with salt and pepper, fill your pancakes and bake in exactly the same way as for Ratatouille Pancakes (opposite).

SPINACH AND ONION FILLING

Serves 2

Basic recipes: Basic Pancake Mixture (page 36); Béchamel Sauce (page 7)

1½ lb (675 g) spinach

2 large onions

2 oz (50 g) butter

¼ pint (150 ml) béchamel sauce

ground nutmeg

4 pancakes

salt and pepper

Wash and cook the spinach. Meanwhile peel and chop the onions and soften them in butter in a covered pan for 10 minutes, being careful not to brown them. Drain and chop the spinach and mix with the onions. Mix into the béchamel and season to taste with nutmeg, salt and pepper. Fill the pancakes and bake in exactly the same way as for Ratatouille Pancakes (opposite).

TARTE AU MOUTARDE

Serves 4

Basic recipe: Pastry (page 6)

9-inch (23 cm) flan case, baked blind (use ⅔ quantity of the basic recipe)

3 tablespoons (3 × 15 ml spoon) Dijon mustard

4 oz (100 g) Gruyère cheese, grated

8 oz (226 g) can of tomatoes

3 egg yolks

⅓ pint (200 ml) double cream

salt and pepper

Oven temperature:
Gas Mark 3/325°F/170°C

I love this unusual pie – it's not at all like the usual quiches, and the runny cheese inside it next to the sharpness of the mustard makes it irresistible.

Spread the bottom of the pastry shell with the mustard. Cover with the grated cheese and top with the tomatoes, drained and chopped. Beat the egg yolks and mix in the cream. Season with salt and pepper and pour into the pie shell. Bake for 1 hour. Leave to rest for 5–10 minutes before eating.

EGG AND SPINACH PIE

Serves 4

Basic recipe: Pastry (page 6)

9-inch (23 cm) flan case, baked blind (use ⅔ quantity of the basic recipe)

1½ lb (675 g) cooked spinach

4 eggs

4 tablespoons (4 × 15 ml spoon) thick cream

1½ oz (40 g) cheese, grated

1½ oz (40 g) breadcrumbs

butter

salt and pepper

Oven temperature:
Gas Mark 5/375°F/190°C

This is totally different from a quiche. The eggs set like poached eggs in their bed of spinach, to make one of my favourite lunch dishes.

Put the chopped spinach in the bottom of the pastry case and make four little nests into which you break the eggs. Season them with salt and pepper and put a spoonful of cream on top of each one. Mix the cheese with the breadcrumbs, season with salt and pepper and cover the eggs and spinach. Dot with butter and bake for 10–15 minutes. Finish for half a minute under a hot grill and serve immediately.

Egg and Spinach Pie
Tarte au Moutarde

CORN PANCAKES

Makes 10

7 oz (200 g) can of
sweetcorn

1 large egg (size 1)

1 oz (25 g) plain flour

5 tablespoons (5 × 15 ml
spoon) top of the milk

butter for frying

*This and the following recipe are for pancakes with a
difference: they are quite substantial in themselves and
require no fillings. They are delicious with egg and
cheese dishes in particular, and also go very well with
curries and stuffed vegetables. Or try giving them to
the kids for supper, fresh from the pan with lavish
helpings of butter!*

Liquidise all the ingredients to a batter, which
will still have little chunks of sweetcorn in it.
Chill for a minimum of two hours. Grease a
heavy frying pan very lightly with butter, and
cook 2 tablespoons (2 × 15 ml spoon) of the
mixture at a time as for drop–scones, so that they
are golden brown on both sides.

POTATO PANCAKES

Makes 6

3 medium-size potatoes

2 tablespoons (2 × 15 ml
spoon) dry breadcrumbs

2 tablespoons (2 × 15 ml
spoon) double cream

2 eggs

1 small onion, grated

vegetable oil for frying

salt and pepper

Peel and grate the potatoes and mix with the
breadcrumbs and cream. Lightly beat the eggs
and mix in, and season with salt, pepper and
grated onion. Stir well, and then drop spoonfuls
into hot oil in a shallow frying pan, and cook for
about 5 minutes on each side until they are
golden and crisp.

ASPARAGUS AND MUSHROOM FLAN

Serves 4

Basic recipe: Pastry (page 6)

10 oz (275 g) can of
asparagus spears or 8 oz
(225 g) fresh asparagus

8-inch (20 cm) flan case,
baked blind

1 oz (25 g) butter

1 small onion, sliced

4 oz (100 g) mushrooms,
sliced

2 eggs

⅓ pint (200 ml) milk

2 oz (50 g) Cheddar cheese,
grated

salt and pepper

Oven temperature:
Gas Mark 6/400°F/200°C

This is a recipe for a rather special occasion because asparagus isn't cheap, whether fresh or canned. But it makes a lovely lunch dish served with a crisp lettuce and avocado salad, and a bottle of chilled Moselle.

Lay the asparagus spears over the bottom of the flan case. Melt the butter and cook the sliced onion in it until it has softened a little. Then add the sliced mushrooms and cook them briefly so that they are still slightly crisp. Spread this mixture over the asparagus. Beat the eggs with the milk, season to taste and pour into the pie dish. Sprinkle with the grated cheese and bake for 25 minutes.

MUSHROOM AND CORIANDER VOL-AU-VENTS

Serves 4

Basic recipe: Béchamel Sauce (page 7)

6 oz (175 g) mushrooms

2 oz (50 g) butter

a medium-size bunch of
coriander, chopped finely

¼ pint (150 ml) thick
béchamel

12 medium-size frozen vol-
au-vent cases, cooked as
instructed on the packet

salt and pepper

Oven temperature:
Gas Mark 4/350°F/180°C

Frozen puff pastry vol-au-vent cases cook up very successfully, and are a simple way of making a light and elegant meal. Like pancakes, there is no end to the variety of fillings that you can use, but to my mind this recipe and the four that follow are among the tastiest.

Chop the mushrooms and cook in the butter for 4–5 minutes. Add the finely chopped coriander and cook for another minute. Liquidise to a purée with a little of the béchamel. Stir this purée into the rest of the béchamel and season to taste with salt and pepper. Cool. Fill the pre-cooked vol-au-vent cases with the mixture and heat through in a moderate oven, for 15 minutes.

43

LEEK PURÉE FILLING

Fills 12 medium-size vol-au-vent cases

Basic recipe: Béchamel Sauce (page 7)

2 lb (900 g) leeks

¼ pint (150 ml) thick béchamel sauce

a knob of butter

salt and pepper

Cook the trimmed and washed leeks, and liquidise with a little of their cooking liquid and the béchamel to make a fairly thick purée. Add a knob of butter and season to taste. Cook as for Mushroom and Coriander Vol-au-vents (page 43).

MUSHROOM, CELERY AND PEANUT FILLING

Fills 12 medium-size vol-au-vent cases

Basic recipe: Béchamel Sauce (page 7)

6 oz (175 g) mushrooms

2 oz (50 g) butter

4 celery sticks

2 oz (50 g) peanuts

parsley

½ pint (300 ml) thick béchamel sauce

salt and pepper

Chop the mushrooms very finely and cook in the butter with the finely sliced celery until both are soft, about 5 minutes. Chop the peanuts coarsely and the parsley finely and add to the mixture. Stir in the béchamel and season with salt and pepper. Cook as for Mushroom and Coriander Vol-au-vents (page 43).

ASPARAGUS FILLING

Fills 12 medium-size vol-au-vent cases

Basic recipe: Béchamel Sauce (page 7)

3 shallots

1 oz (25 g) butter

10 oz (275 g) can of asparagus

½ pint (300 ml) thick béchamel sauce

a little cream

salt and pepper

Slice the shallots and soften in the melted butter for 3 minutes. Chop the asparagus into ½-inch (1 cm) lengths and add with the shallots to the béchamel. Thin out with a little cream and season to taste with salt and pepper. Cook as for Mushroom and Coriander Vol-au-vents (page 43).

Three fillings for vol-au-vents: Leek Purée; Mushroom, Celery and Peanut; Asparagus

SOUBISE FILLING

Fills 12 medium-size vol-au-vent cases

Basic recipe: Béchamel Sauce (page 7)

1 lb (450 g) onions	Slice the onions finely and cook them in the melted butter, covered, over a very gentle heat, stirring from time to time until they are soft and sweet but not browned. This will take 15–20 minutes. Add to the béchamel and season to taste with nutmeg, salt and pepper. Cook as for Mushroom and Coriander Vol-au-vents (page 43).
3 oz (75 g) butter	
½ pint (300 ml) thick béchamel sauce	
nutmeg	
salt and pepper	

EGG FLAN WITH JERUSALEM ARTICHOKES

Serves 4

Basic recipe: Pastry (page 6)

1 lb (450 g) jerusalem artichokes	*This is one of my favourite quick supper dishes – it is a really unusual and delicious combination. I like to serve it with pasta and a selection of salads.*
2 oz (50 g) butter	Peel and cook the artichokes 'al dente', then cool and dice them. Melt half the butter in a frying pan and let it get really hot. When it turns nut brown sauté the artichokes quickly. Remove and keep warm. Season the eggs with salt and pepper, add the milk or cream, and scramble lightly in the rest of the butter, adding the artichokes half-way through the cooking. Pile into the warm pastry case and garnish with chopped parsley. Serve immediately.
4 large eggs (size 1–2), beaten	
2 tablespoons (2 × 15 ml spoon) milk or cream	
8-inch (20 cm) flan case, baked blind	
salt and pepper	
To garnish:	
chopped parsley	

STILTON TART

Basic recipe: Pastry (page 6)

1 oz (25 g) butter

2 tablespoons (2 × 15 ml spoon) plain flour

½ pint (300 ml) milk

8 oz (225 g) Stilton cheese, crumbled

2 tablespoons (2 × 15 ml spoon) Dijon mustard

ground mace

3 eggs

2 × 8-inch (20 cm) pastry shells, baked blind

salt and pepper

Oven temperatures:
Gas Mark 7/425°F/220°C
Gas Mark 6/400°F/200°C

The idea for this recipe came to me one January when I surveyed the usual Christmas leftovers: there was a large piece of rejected Stilton, still delicious, but unwanted after all the excesses of the festivities. So I decided to disguise it.

Melt the butter and stir in the flour. Add the milk gradually, stirring until the sauce thickens. Simmer gently for 5 minutes and then add the crumbled Stilton and the mustard. Stir until they are well amalgamated, and then season to taste with salt, pepper and ground mace. Cool a little. Separate the eggs and beat the whites until stiff. Beat the yolks, stir into the cheese mixture, and then fold in the whites. Pour into the pastry cases and bake for 5 minutes at the higher setting, and then for about 10–12 minutes at the lower setting, until wholly set and a knife comes out clean from the middle. Serve at once.

POTATO AND ONION PIE

1 lb (450 g) potatoes

butter

milk

1 egg

¼ pint (150 ml) top of the milk

1 small onion

salt and pepper

Oven temperature:
Gas Mark 5/375°F/190°C

Laughably simple though this seems, it is extraordinarily good, and makes the most satisfying of supper dishes on cold evenings. Serve perhaps with a mixture of vegetables, such as beetroot and green peas, or cauliflower and mushrooms.

Boil the potatoes and mash them with butter and milk, and season with salt and pepper. Butter an 8-inch (20 cm) flan tin and make a border around the edge with the mashed potatoes. Beat the egg, mix in the top of the milk and then add the chopped onion. Season to taste and pour into the middle of the potato ring. Bake for 20 minutes until the centre is puffed and golden.

EGG, CHEESE AND PASTA DISHES

CHEESE FONDUE

Serves 4

2 teaspoons (2 × 5 ml spoon) cornflour

1 teaspoon (5 ml spoon) dry mustard

½ pint (300 ml) dry cider

1 oz (25 g) butter

1 lb (450 g) Cheddar cheese, grated

pepper

I always enjoy a meal around a fondue pot: it is informal, relaxed, and there is an element of sharing that is absent from more elegant styles of eating! Serve this with little squares of fresh bread and a platter of crudités – which could include all or some of the following: cucumber, radishes, tomatoes, lightly cooked courgettes, celery, small button mushrooms, raw carrots, cooked beetroot, waxy new potatoes, broccoli spears – and anything else that inspires you!

Blend the cornflour, mustard and pepper to a smooth cream with a little of the cider. Set aside. Melt the butter in a fondue pot, add the cheese and remaining cider, and heat gently, stirring until it is smooth. Add the flour mixture, turn up the heat a little and stir until it thickens. Bubble gently over the flame of the fondue burner and dip the suggested vegetables and little squares of bread in the cheesy mixture. It is filling – but delicious!

Cheese Fondue

CAULIFLOWER CHEESE SOUFFLÉ

Serves 4

half a medium-size cauliflower

1½ oz (40 g) butter, plus extra for greasing

2 tablespoons (2 × 15 ml spoon) plain flour

¼ pint (150 ml) milk

nutmeg

4 oz (100 g) Cheddar cheese, grated

3 large eggs (size 1)

salt and pepper

Oven temperature:
Gas Mark 6/400°F/200°C

Because the cauliflower is cooked with the soufflé this dish is almost a meal in itself. For large appetites all it needs is some little boiled potatoes to go with it. It is a good family dish – I find that the young ones like it as much as their seniors.

Divide the cauliflower into small florets and lightly boil for 3 minutes so that they are cooked but still crisp. Melt the butter, stir in the flour and add the milk gradually over a gentle heat, stirring all the time until the mixture is smooth and thick. Season to taste with salt, pepper and nutmeg. Stir in the cheese, let it amalgamate, and then remove from the heat. Separate the eggs. Add the yolks to the cheese mixture, stir well and stir in the cauliflower. Beat the whites until they are stiff and fold carefully into the mixture. Put in a well greased soufflé dish and cook for 20–25 minutes until well risen and still slightly creamy inside.

ONION OMELETTE

1 lb (450 g) onions

4 oz (100 g) butter

nutmeg

6 eggs

5 fl oz (150 ml) carton of single cream

salt and pepper

Onions cooked very slowly in butter are nectar: they turn sweet and soft and quite lose the bite of the vegetable in its raw state, or the strong taste of quickly fried, browned onions. The idea for making an omelette filled with these sweet onions comes from a tiny 'café routier' in France where we stopped once for a simple, but most delicious, travellers' meal. Serve with new potatoes, broccoli and a crisp green salad.

Peel and slice the onions very finely. Melt the butter in a fairly deep pan and cook the onion in it over a very low heat, covered, until softened but not browned, for about 15–20 minutes. Stir occasionally, and when they are sweet and soft they are ready. Season to taste with salt, pepper and ground nutmeg.

Beat the eggs well and stir in the cream. Season with more salt and pepper. Make the omelette in the usual way and use the onion for the filling.

AUBERGINES WITH PASTA AND CHEESE

Serves 6

2 medium-size aubergines

olive oil, for frying

8 oz (225 g) pasta shapes

½ pint (300 ml) tomato sauce made with 3 tablespoons (3 × 15 ml spoon) tomato purée and water

8 oz (225 g) strong cheese, grated

1 clove of garlic, crushed

salt and pepper

Oven temperature:
Gas Mark 4/350°F/180°C

This is a kind of Italian answer to moussaka, and is deliciously rich and warming food. Serve it up as a meal in its own right, with a green salad.

Cut the aubergines into fairly thin slices and sprinkle them with salt. Let them sweat for 30 minutes, and then wipe them dry. Cook in olive oil – they absorb it well, so you will need quite a lot – until they are soft and slightly browned. Cook the pasta 'al dente'. Put layers in a baking dish of the tomato sauce, sliced aubergine, pasta and grated cheese, seasoning with garlic, salt and pepper as you go. Finish with a layer of the cheese and bake for 25 minutes.

Aubergines with Pasta and Cheese

Poached Eggs en Cho[...]

Cannelloni with Mushrooms
and Basil

CANNELLONI WITH MUSHROOMS AND BASIL

Basic recipe: Béchamel Sauce (page 7)

6 oz (175 g) mushrooms

2 oz (50 g) butter, plus a little extra for greasing

4 oz (100 g) frozen or fresh peas

a large bunch of fresh basil

¼ pint (150 ml) thick béchamel sauce

8 cannelloni tubes

4 oz (100 g) Cheddar cheese, grated

salt and pepper

Oven temperature:
Gas Mark 5/375°F/190°C

You can improvise with all kinds of stuffings for pasta, rather as you can with pancakes – they invariably make appetising and popular meals. Here the taste of basil evokes Italian sunshine, and goes excellently with the mushrooms and peas. A winner with all age groups!

Chop the mushrooms small and cook them in the hot butter until they have softened a little. Cook the peas and chop the basil finely. Add all the vegetables to the béchamel sauce. Mix well and season to taste. Cook the cannelloni as instructed on the packet and stuff with the mixture. Put them into a well greased ovenproof dish, smother with the grated cheese and heat thoroughly for 15–20 minutes until the cheese has browned.

POACHED EGGS EN CHOUX

Makes 6 large puffs

Basic recipe: Béchamel Sauce (page 7)

For the choux puffs:

2 oz (50 g) butter

5 tablespoons (5 × 15 ml spoon) water

2 oz (50 g) plain flour

3 eggs

salt

For the cheese sauce:

3 oz (75 g) Gruyère cheese, grated

½ pint (300 ml) béchamel sauce

lots of black pepper

a little cream

6 eggs for the filling

Oven temperature:
Gas Mark 7/425°F/220°C

Choux puffs are far easier to make than they appear, and they always look as if hours of work had been spent on making them. Filled with a poached egg and covered with a light cheese sauce, they make an excellent dish.

To make the puffs, melt the butter with the water and stir in the sifted flour and salt. Mix thoroughly until completely amalgamated. Then, off the heat, beat in the eggs with a wooden spoon, one at a time, until the mixture is glossy and homogeneous.

Place in tablespoons on a well greased baking dish (set well apart because they will blow up like balloons) and cook for 25 minutes. To make the sauce, stir the cheese into the béchamel over a low heat until it melts. Season with black pepper and thin out with a little cream.

Poach one egg per person. Slit the puffs along the side and slip the eggs in. Cover with the cheese sauce and put with care under a hot grill for a few seconds so that the sauce browns slightly. Serve immediately.

GOUGÈRE

2 oz (50 g) butter, plus a little extra for greasing

½ pint (300 ml) milk, plus a little extra for glazing

4 oz (100 g) flour

4 eggs

3 oz (75 g) Gruyère cheese, diced

salt and pepper

Oven temperature:
Gas Mark 5/375°F/190°C

Gougère makes a spectacular and wholesome dish, filled with any of the stuffings suggested below. It is rich, and a little goes a long way, so just serve it with a salad of your choice and a hearty red wine.

Cut the butter into small pieces and put in the milk with some salt and pepper and bring to the boil. Pour in the sifted flour and stir until you have a thick smooth paste which comes away cleanly from the sides of the pan. Remove from the heat and stir in the eggs one at a time, thoroughly amalgamating each one. When the mixture is thick and shiny, add the diced cheese and leave to cool.

Make a ring of the mixture on a well-greased baking tray, by placing spoonfuls of the mixture in a circle about 8 inches (20 cm) in diameter, leaving a hole in the centre. Brush with milk and bake for 45 minutes. When cool, stuff the centre of the ring with a filling of your choice.

SUGGESTED FILLINGS FOR GOUGÈRE

Any of the pancake fillings on pages 38–39
Stir-fried beansprouts with lettuce
Courgettes in Soubise sauce (page 46)
Skinned, chopped tomatoes cooked in butter with herbs
Creamed mushrooms
Cauliflower cheese

Gougère filled with stir-fried beansprouts and lettuce

NOODLES WITH MUSHROOMS

Serves 4

12 oz (350 g) noodles

2 eggs

3 oz (75 g) butter

2 tablespoons (2 × 15 ml spoon) top of the milk

8 oz (225 g) mushrooms

juice of ½ lemon

breadcrumbs

salt and pepper

Oven temperature:
Gas Mark 5/375°F/190°C

This makes a delicious dish on its own, is popular with children, and also makes a lovely accompaniment to the Vegetable Kebabs on page 32.

Boil the noodles, drain and rinse them very quickly in cold water and leave to drain again. Beat the eggs with 1 oz (25 g) butter and the milk and stir them into the pasta. Season. Chop the mushrooms and cook in 1 oz (25 g) butter until softened; season with salt, pepper and lemon juice. Put half of the noodles on the bottom of a greased baking dish, cover with the mushrooms and top with the rest of the noodles. Cover with breadcrumbs, dot lavishly with the rest of the butter and bake for 15 minutes.

GIANFRANCO'S PASTA SALAD

Serves 6

3 large cloves of garlic

1 large red pepper

1 large green pepper

6 celery sticks

3 carrots

a large bunch of parsley

½ pint (300 ml) good olive oil

12 oz (350 g) pasta shapes, cooked 'al dente' and allowed to cool a little

salt and pepper

This pasta salad was given to me by the wife of an Italian friend at a summer party: it was so beautiful that I couldn't resist eating more and more of it! The salad really is superb, and is best eaten the day after it is made so that all the tastes permeate the pasta. Don't be afraid to use masses of garlic – the more there is the more delicious the mixture will be.

Chop the garlic very finely. Grill and skin the peppers; slice them thinly and cut the slices into short lengths. Slice and chop the celery and carrots finely, and chop the parsley very small. Soak all the vegetables and herbs in the olive oil and season to taste with salt and pepper. Dress the pasta, still warm, with this mixture and toss well, turning it regularly until you are ready to serve it.

CHEESE CROQUETTES

8 oz (225 g) cheese such as Caerphilly or Cheshire, grated

1 tablespoon (15 ml spoon) plain flour, plus a little extra for rolling

2 eggs, beaten

1 teaspoon (5 ml spoon) chopped parsley

a pinch of mace

fat for deep frying

These delectable morsels turn out crisp on the outside and gooey with melted cheese on the inside. They are lovely as a snack on their own with a salad, or as an accompaniment to any vegetable or pasta dish.

Work to an even paste the cheese, flour, beaten eggs, parsley and mace. Form into ½-inch (1 cm) rolls about 4 inches (10 cm) long, roll in flour and fry in deep hot fat until golden all over and crisp on the outside.

CHEESE-STUFFED TOMATOES

4 medium-size tomatoes

4 oz (100 g) Cheddar cheese, grated

French mustard (optional)

pepper

Oven temperature:
Gas Mark 5/375°F/190°C

These are delicious either on toast, as a snack lunch, or as an accompaniment to the Lentil Loaf on page 22. Personally I think that cheese and pulses are irresistible together.

Cut a slice off the top of the tomatoes and scoop out the flesh inside, leaving them hollow. Grate the cheese finely and season with lots of black pepper and a little French mustard if you like it. Pack inside the hollowed-out tomatoes, put the 'lids' back on top and bake for 15–20 minutes.

TAGLIATELLE WITH HERB SAUCE

1 rounded tablespoon (1–2 × 15 ml spoon) desiccated coconut

½ pint (300 ml) boiling water

2 rounded tablespoons (2–3 × 15 ml spoon) salted peanuts

½ tablespoon (½ × 15 ml spoon) coriander seeds

1 teaspoon (5 ml spoon) turmeric

1 rounded tablespoon (1–2 × 15 ml spoon) fresh basil or coriander

1 onion

1 oz (25 g) butter or vegetable margarine

1 tablespoon (15 ml spoon) plain flour

1 lb (450 g) tagliatelle cooked 'al dente'

The simplicity of this dish belies its great taste: the fragrance of fresh herbs is quite wonderful with the pasta. This recipe is beautifully quick to make, and can be a starter served in small quantities, or a main course with a large mixed salad.

Steep the coconut in the boiling water for 10 minutes, and then strain it. Liquidise the nuts, herbs and spices in this coconut milk so that they are well blended. Chop the onion and soften it in the butter or margarine. Stir in the flour and add the liquidised mixture slowly, stirring while the sauce thickens. Heat through and pour over the prepared tagliatelle.

Tagliatelle with Herb Sauce

FETTUCCINE WITH GARLIC AND CORIANDER

Serves 4

12 oz (350 g) fettuccine

5 fl oz (150 ml) olive oil

2 cloves of garlic, crushed

a bunch of fresh coriander, chopped finely

2 oz (50 g) pine kernels

salt and pepper

To garnish:

grated parmesan cheese

Pasta combined with garlic, olive oil, fresh coriander leaves and pine kernels is food for the gods. Good for the waistline it may not be, but being so sublime it must be good for the soul!

Cook the fettuccine 'al dente'. Combine the oil with the garlic and coriander and season with plenty of salt and pepper. Pour over the pasta and toss thoroughly, then sprinkle the pine kernels over and serve on hot plates, sprinkled with the parmesan.

NOODLES AND CHEESE OMELETTE

Serves 4

4 spring onions, chopped finely

½ oz (15 g) butter

3 large eggs (size 1–2), beaten

a little milk or cream

2 tablespoons (2 × 15 ml spoon) sesame oil

2 oz (50 g) thin egg noodles, cooked and chopped

2 oz (50 g) Edam cheese, grated

This is a delicious, quick and simple lunch or supper dish, quite substantial in its own right and best, I think, with a crisp, green salad and a glass of rosé wine.

Cook the spring onions in the butter to soften them slightly. Remove from the pan. Mix the eggs with a little milk or cream, and season with salt and pepper. Heat the sesame oil in the pan and start to make the omelette. Half-way through the cooking add the spring onions, cheese and chopped noodles. When set, fold it in half and serve immediately.

SPICY NOODLES

4 oz (100 g) noodles

6 spring onions, sliced very finely

2 oz (50 g) crunchy peanut butter

1 teaspoon (5 ml spoon) garam masala

1 large clove of garlic, crushed

3 tablespoons (3 × 15 ml spoon) sesame oil

2 tablespoons (2 × 15 ml spoon) soy sauce

The tastes in this sauce are gorgeous – quite strong and distinctive, but an excellent foil to the soft bland noodles. They go beautifully with the Tomato Soufflé below, and the Spinach and Mushroom Salad on page 86.

Cook the noodles and prepare the spring onions. Blend the rest of the ingredients to a paste, and pour over the hot, drained noodles. Sprinkle in the spring onions and toss thoroughly. Serve at once.

TOMATO SOUFFLÉ

Serves 4

Basic recipe: Béchamel Sauce (page 7)

1½ lb (675 g) ripe tomatoes

1 oz (25 g) butter

1 tablespoon (15 ml spoon) tomato purée

¼ pint (150 ml) béchamel sauce

nutmeg

4 eggs, separated

1 oz (25 g) parmesan cheese, grated

salt and pepper

Oven temperature:
Gas Mark 7/425°F/220°C

This is a lovely summery dish: light, refreshing, and tasty. It is also a useful variation in times of glut, late in summer when tomatoes are two a penny. Serve it with a fresh green salad sprinkled with chopped fresh herbs, little new potatoes and Granary bread – it makes a meal to remember.

Chop the tomatoes and cook in the butter until they are softened. Sieve, and add with the tomato purée to the béchamel. Season with nutmeg, salt and pepper. Beat and add the egg yolks and stir in well. Beat the egg whites until very stiff, fold them carefully into the mixture and sprinkle with the parmesan. Cook for 20–25 minutes until risen and set, but still a little runny in the centre.

EGGS WITH PEPPERS

2 peppers, one red and one green

4 tablespoons (4 × 15 ml spoon) good olive oil

garlic to taste, sliced finely

4 eggs

salt and black pepper

This is one of my favourite simple dishes – it takes only a matter of minutes to prepare but is richly rewarding, with exotic flavours and textures. But use only the very best olive oil! Serve with mashed potatoes and a green salad, and a glass of robust red wine.

Clean, de-seed and slice the peppers into 1-inch (2.5 cm) thick slices. Heat the oil gently in a frying pan and add the peppers, stirring for a minute or two until they are warmed through. Add the finely sliced garlic, salt, and lots of black pepper, mix together and cover with a lid. Cook very gently for 15 minutes, stirring from time to time. Then break the eggs gently into the pan and let them cook through. Serve immediately.

Eggs with Peppers

EGG AND LETTUCE GRATIN

Serves 4

Basic recipe: Béchamel Sauce (page 7)

2 lettuces, shredded

6 soft-boiled eggs

¾ pint (450 ml) béchamel sauce, made with half cream and half milk

masses of fresh chives, chopped finely

2 oz (50 g) fresh breadcrumbs

oil for frying

Oven temperature:
Gas Mark 7/425°F/220°C

Cooked lettuce is one of the most underestimated vegetables in the Western hemisphere: very light cooking brings out its delicate flavour, and it makes a delicious base for soft-boiled eggs. Serve the dish with buttered new potatoes and it is a meal in itself.

Cover the bottom of a ovenproof dish with the shredded lettuce. Halve the eggs and place on top. Cover with the béchamel, into which you have stirred masses of finely chopped chives. Bake for 10 minutes. Meanwhile, fry the breadcrumbs until golden. Sprinkle them over the top and serve at once.

PASTA WITH AUBERGINE SAUCE

Serves 4

2 medium-size aubergines

olive oil

4 tomatoes, skinned and chopped finely

1 clove of garlic, crushed

a small bunch of fresh basil, chopped

12 oz (350 g) noodles or pasta shapes, cooked 'al dente'

2 oz (50 g) grated parmesan cheese

salt and pepper

Of all the simple sauces you can serve with pasta this is one of my favourites. It has style and originality, and all the strong flavours of the Mediterranean.

Slice the aubergines thinly and cut into ¼-inch (5 mm) cubes. Cook gently in olive oil (they will absorb quite a lot) until they begin to soften, about 5 minutes, and then add the skinned and finely chopped tomatoes, the crushed garlic, salt and pepper. Cook for a further 5 minutes and then add the chopped basil leaves. Mix with the cooked, well drained pasta and serve sprinkled with parmesan.

POACHED EGGS INDIAN STYLE

4 oz (100 g) basmati rice

For the curry sauce:

1 small onion

1 oz (25 g) butter

1–2 teaspoons (1–2 × 5 ml spoon) garam masala, according to taste

1 tablespoon (15 ml spoon) plain flour

¼ pint (150 ml) stock

a little cream or top of the milk

2 large tomatoes

4 eggs

salt and pepper

The soft blandness of a poached egg sitting on a bed of rice and sliced tomatoes is offset by the spiciness of a light curry sauce: one of the best supper dishes I know, served with cauliflower and a leafy, herby salad.

Cook the rice and keep it warm whilst you make the curry sauce, as follows. Peel and chop the onion finely, and cook in the butter until softened but not browned. Stir in the garam masala, and then the flour, and gradually add the stock until it thickens. Stir in a little cream or top of the milk and it is ready.

Slice the tomatoes and put them in the bottom of a baking dish. Season, and grill until softened a little. Cover with the cooked rice, top with the poached eggs and smother with the curry sauce. Serve immediately.

VEGETABLE SIDE DISHES AND SALADS

FRIED RICE MEMSAHIB

Pictured on page 29 | Serves 2

1 onion

1 oz (25 g) butter or
vegetable margarine

sesame oil

4 oz (100 g) basmati rice,
rinsed but uncooked

garlic

2 teaspoons (2 × 5 ml
spoon) garam masala

½–¾ pint (300–450 ml)
stock

2 oz (50 g) frozen peas

2 celery sticks, chopped
finely

*Inspired by India, this tasty, slightly spiced rice is
wonderful with the Vegetable Kebabs on page 32.*

Chop the onion and soften it in the melted fat
and sesame oil. Add the rinsed rice and stir until
well coated. Crush a little garlic into the pan and
sprinkle over the garam masala. Stir for a minute
or two, and then gradually add the stock,
stirring until it is absorbed by the rice. Add the
peas and celery and stir until all are cooked.
Serve at once.

DHAL

Pictured on page 29

Serves 4

8 oz (225 g) green lentils, soaked overnight

a pinch of turmeric

1 large onion, chopped

1 bay leaf

2-inch piece of root ginger

1 tablespoon (15 ml spoon) chopped curry leaves or parsley

1 fresh green chilli, chopped

4 tablespoons (4 × 15 ml spoon) olive oil

3 large cloves of garlic, crushed

½ teaspoon (2.5 ml spoon) cumin seeds, crushed

¼ teaspoon (1.25 ml spoon) mustard seeds, crushed

1 or 2 dried chillies (optional)

8 oz (226 g) can of tomatoes, drained and chopped

Delicately spiced, lentils can be food for the gods. Try this Indian recipe for its beautiful flavour, with or without chillies, according to taste. Then try it mixed with any of the vegetables suggested below, for a delicious meal all out of one bowl – it needs only bread or chapati to go with it.

Put the lentils, turmeric, onion, bay leaf, ginger, curry leaves or parsley, fresh chilli and 1 tablespoon (15 ml spoon) oil in a pan with enough water to cover. Bring to the boil and simmer, covered, over a gentle heat for about 45 minutes until the lentils are cooked. Add a little extra water if the lentils start to stick. Warm the remaining oil and cook the crushed garlic in it until slightly browned. Add the spices and cook a further few minutes. Stir in the chopped tomatoes, heat through, and stir in the cooked lentils. Heat through and bubble over a gentle heat for 5–10 minutes before serving.

Dhal variations: add sliced courgettes to dhal, or radishes, mushrooms, cauliflower florets, peas, nuts, okra, green beans or spinach – the variations are endless. Just heat through together and you have a nutritious and delicious meal.

VEGETABLE SALAD WITH TARRAGON MAYONNAISE

4 oz (100 g) young carrots
4 oz (100 g) broccoli, cooked 'al dente'
4 oz (100 g) french beans, cooked 'al dente'
4 oz (100 g) peas, cooked 'al dente'
4 oz (100 g) lentils, soaked overnight and cooked
2 oz (50 g) beansprouts
3 oz (75 g) courgettes, sliced thinly
a large bunch of tarragon
6 tablespoons (6 × 15 ml spoon) mayonnaise
lemon juice
salt and pepper

Tarragon is one of the best herbs to go with vegetables, so use it lavishly! This delicious salad can be a meal in its own right, or an addition to a salad buffet table. Try it also with tarragon vinaigrette – it's hard to choose between them!

Peel and dice the carrots, and cut the broccoli and french beans into 1-inch (2 cm) lengths. Put with all the rest of the vegetables in a salad bowl. Chop the tarragon very finely and mix into the mayonnaise. Dress the vegetables with it, season to taste with salt and pepper and lemon juice, and it is ready to serve.

DEEP-FRIED CABBAGE

Deep-frying cabbage brings out its strong flavour and the end result is not unlike crisply fried onions, although less pungent. It is really delicious, and a superb side vegetable for egg dishes.

Just shred as much cabbage as you require and deep-fry at chip heat until crisp and golden. Drain on kitchen paper, sprinkle with salt and serve hot.

LETTUCE WITH CREAM

1 lb (450 g) soft lettuce
leaves

3 oz (75 g) butter

¼–½ pint (150–300 ml)
double cream

1 small onion, grated

salt and freshly ground black
pepper

To garnish:

3 slices of bread, cubed and
fried into croûtons

*Lightly cooked, lettuce has a beautifully nutty
flavour, and lends itself to all kinds of experiments.
Try this combination with butter and cream, which,
served with croûtons, is almost a meal in itself.*

Shred the lettuce leaves and cook in the melted
butter over a gentle heat until wilted. Season
with salt, reduce the heat further and cover the
pan. Cook for a further 5 minutes and then add
the cream, grated onion and pepper and stir
well. Heat through and serve with the croûtons.

VEGETABLE GRATIN WITH CUCUMBER

Serves 6

1 large cucumber

a large bunch of spring
onions, chopped

half a small cauliflower, cut
into small florets

1 oz (25 g) butter

4 oz (100 g) cheese, grated

1 oz (25 g) breadcrumbs

salt and pepper

Oven temperature:
Gas Mark 4/350°F/180°C

*This is an original way of dealing with cucumber,
which is delicious hot, and it makes a welcome change
from salads when the cucumber season is at its height.*

Quarter the unpeeled cucumber and then cut
each quarter into ¼-inch (5 mm) slices. Fry the
spring onions and cauliflower in the butter for 5
minutes. Put the cucumber in the bottom of an
ovenproof dish, put the fried mixture over the
top and sprinkle with salt and pepper.
  Mix the cheese with the breadcrumbs and put
over the top. Bake for 30 minutes.

SWEET AND SOUR BABY ONIONS

Serves 4

1 lb (450 g) small onions

2 tablespoons (2 × 15 ml spoon) olive oil

3 cloves

1 bay leaf

4 tablespoons (4 × 15 ml spoon) vinegar

2 tablespoons (2 × 15 ml spoon) sugar

salt

This is definitely my favourite way of eating little onions. Simple to make, it is a lovely change from more conventional ways of cooking them, and can be eaten hot or cold.

Boil the onions in their skins for 5–8 minutes, until soft. Cool and peel them. Put into a pan with the olive oil, cloves, bay leaf and salt and simmer very gently for 5 minutes more. Add the vinegar and sugar and cook until the sauce begins to go syrupy.

RUNNER BEANS WITH ALMONDS

Serves 4

1½ lb (675 g) runner beans

4 oz (100 g) butter or vegetable margarine

4 oz (100 g) blanched almonds

salt and pepper

During the glut of runner beans in the summer it is often difficult to think of new ways of presenting them. This recipe is sumptuous and memorable.

Top, tail and finely slice the beans and blanch them in boiling water for 5 minutes. Drain them and return to the pan with 3 oz (75 g) of the fat. Cover and simmer gently until cooked through. Brown the almonds in the rest of the fat and stir into the beans. Add salt and pepper to taste and serve very hot.

Sweet and Sour Baby Onion.
Runner Beans with Almond

MASHED POTATO SPECIAL

Serves 4

1 lb (450 g) potatoes, peeled

8 oz (225 g) carrots

a large bunch of sorrel

butter and milk

salt and pepper

There are many ways to ring the changes with mashed potatoes. They combine so well with root vegetables – either with carrots, as in this recipe, or with celeriac, salsify, swedes or turnips. Here, sorrel adds a refreshing sharpness to the root vegetables. Put poached eggs on this purée for a lovely, easy supper.

Boil the potatoes with the carrots. Meanwhile wash the sorrel and cook it in its own juices until completely soft. Mash the potatoes together with the carrots, adding enough butter and milk to make a soft purée. Stir in the sorrel, mix well, and season to taste with salt and masses of ground black pepper.

BAKED CHICORY

Serves 4

1 lb (450 g) chicory

4 oz (100 g) butter

½ teaspoon (2.5 ml spoon) salt

½ teaspoon (2.5 ml spoon) sugar

juice of 1 lemon

A wonderful salad leaf raw, chicory is sublime cooked. Rather like lettuce, it changes its flavour completely and in a delicious way.

Separate the chicory leaves from the stem. Melt the butter in a flameproof casserole dish or deep frying pan and toss the leaves in it. Season with salt, sugar, and the juice of the lemon and cover with foil. Cook over a very gentle heat for 10–15 minutes.

SPINACH DAISY

Serves 4

Basic recipe: Béchamel Sauce (page 7)

1 lb (450 g) spinach

8 oz (225 g) mushrooms

4 oz (100 g) butter

1/3 pint (200 ml) thick béchamel sauce

2 oz (50 g) cheese, grated

2 oz (50 g) breadcrumbs

salt and pepper

Oven temperature:
Gas Mark 5/375°F/190°C

This is a dish to delight – a central layer of creamed mushrooms, sandwiched between chopped spinach and a crispy cheese topping to give a contrasting crunch. It melts in the mouth.

Cook the spinach, drain and chop it. Slice the mushrooms and cook them quickly in 3 oz (75 g) butter, and then stir them with their juices into the béchamel sauce. Line the bottom of a soufflé dish with half of the spinach, cover with the creamed mushrooms and top with the rest of the spinach. Mix the grated cheese with the breadcrumbs, season with salt and lots of black pepper, cover the spinach with the mixture and dot with the remaining butter. Bake for 30 minutes.

ROASTED PEPPERS VINAIGRETTE

Serves 4–5

2 large green peppers

2 large red peppers

1 large clove of garlic

6 tablespoons (6 × 15 ml spoon) vinaigrette dressing

The strong colours of this simple salad are as enticing as its rich combination of smells: bright red and dark green strips of peppers flavoured with garlic. It makes a beautiful side salad.

Cut the peppers in half and remove the stalks, seeds and pith. Grill, skin side up, for about 6 minutes under a moderate grill until browned. When soft, cool them and peel off the brown skin. Cut lengthways into thin strips. Crush the garlic into the vinaigrette and pour over the warm peppers in a dish. Leave to marinate until ready to serve.

CORN ROLLS

Serves 2

7 oz (200 g) can of sweetcorn

1 oz (25 g) desiccated coconut

a small piece of root ginger

1 large clove of garlic

a small bunch of fresh coriander leaves

lemon juice

1 oz (25 g) semolina

1 egg yolk, beaten

plain flour

oil for frying

salt and pepper

Looking like little croquettes, these oriental-tasting rolls are delicious with any simple main course, and are also a tasty snack on their own. Make very tiny ones to serve as appetisers.

Liquidise the corn with the coconut, ginger, garlic, coriander, lemon juice and salt. Add the semolina and beaten egg yolk. Shape into four croquettes and chill prior to cooking. Roll in seasoned flour and cook in very hot oil for a few minutes until golden all over.

POMMES DAUPHINE

Makes 24

2 oz (50 g) butter

5 tablespoons (5 × 15 ml spoon) water

2 oz (50 g) plain flour

a pinch of salt

3 medium-size eggs

1 lb (450 g) potatoes, boiled and mashed

ground nutmeg and pepper, to season

oil for deep frying

These are well worth the work they require: delicious golden goodies that melt in the mouth. Serve them with egg or cheese dishes, or with any of the vegetable main courses. And make extra if there are any children around – they love them!

Melt the butter in a pan with the water and stir in the sifted flour and a pinch of salt. Mix very well until completely amalgamated. Then, off the heat, beat in the eggs one at a time with a wooden spoon, until the mixture is glossy and homogeneous.

Stir in the mashed potatoes and mix thoroughly. Add pepper and nutmeg to taste. Deep-fry tablespoons of the mixture, turning until golden and puffed and cooked through.

Corn Rolls
Pommes Dauphine

RED CABBAGE WITH APPLES

Serves 4

1 small red cabbage

3 tablespoons (3 × 15 ml spoon) vinegar

2 oz (50 g) butter or vegetable margarine

2 apples

salt and pepper

Oven temperature:
Gas Mark 3/325°F/170°C

So appetising is this way of cooking red cabbage that I personally could eat it every day through the winter. It is wonderful.

Cut the cabbage into quarters and remove the stalk. Shred the rest finely and put in a casserole with the vinegar, butter or margarine, salt and pepper. Cover with a lid and bake for 1 hour. Then add the chopped apples and cook for a further 30–45 minutes, until both the cabbage and the apples are tender.

BABY BEETROOT WITH FRENCH BEANS

Serves 6

1 lb (450 g) baby beetroot

1 lb (450 g) french beans

good olive oil

pepper

This recipe is ideal for those who grow their own vegetables and who can select tiny, delectable beetroot early in the season, and pick tender french beans before they reach full size. The two make a good marriage.

Cook the beetroot until tender and skin them. Cook the french beans 'al dente'. Heat the oil in a pan and pour it over the two vegetables in a warmed serving dish. Toss well, season with lots of black pepper, and serve.

MUNG BEANS WITH RICE

Serves 4

8 oz (225 g) mung beans

6 oz (175 g) basmati rice

1 bay leaf

1 large onion, chopped finely

2 cloves of garlic, crushed

olive oil

salt and pepper

A simple mixture of subtle flavours, this side dish is lightly seasoned with garlic, and its different textures go beautifully together. You can try the same variations as with Dhal (page 69), to serve it up as a meal in itself: a risotto with a difference!

Boil the mung beans with the rice, bay leaf, finely chopped onion, and salt and pepper. When they are tender drain them, season with crushed garlic and toss in olive oil. Serve hot.

CELERY AND MACARONI SALAD

Serves 4

6 oz (175 g) macaroni

4 oz (100 g) button mushrooms

3 celery sticks

the base of 1 head of celery

4 tablespoons (4 × 15 ml spoon) mayonnaise, thinned with a little milk or lemon juice

garlic and black pepper to taste

To garnish:

1 hard-boiled egg, chopped finely

chopped parsley

There are very few salads as good as this one, and it is a wonderful stand-by for the winter months when the variety of salad ingredients is limited. It is tasty, nourishing and filling, yet crisp and fresh-tasting at the same time.

Cook the macaroni 'al dente' and drain. Cut the mushrooms in half, and chop the celery quite finely. Shred the celery base. Mix the garlic and black pepper into the mayonnaise and toss the cooked macaroni and the vegetables in it. Decorate with the hard-boiled egg and chopped parsley and serve chilled. Like most pasta salads, it is always better the next day!

CHINESE STIR-FRY VEGETABLES

1 lb (450 g) mixed
vegetables, e.g.
beansprouts, mushrooms,
carrots, white cabbage,
celery, peppers, string
beans, cauliflower, broccoli

4 tablespoons (4 × 15 ml
spoon) sesame oil

1 tablespoon (15 ml spoon)
cornflour

5 tablespoons (5 × 15 ml
spoon) water

1 teaspoon (5 ml spoon)
grated fresh ginger

3 tablespoons (3 × 15 ml
spoon) soy sauce

salt

*You can use any variety of vegetables for this dish,
which is best cooked in a wok if possible. It takes only
a few minutes to cook through, so take care not to
overcook, and makes a tasty, light and crunchy side
dish.*

Prepare the vegetables as necessary and chop
into small pieces. Stir-fry in the oil for 3
minutes. Blend the cornflour with the water and
stir in the ginger and salt. Add to the pan and stir
for 2–3 minutes, then add the soy sauce. Mix
well and serve immediately.

Chinese Stir-fry Vegetables

Herbed Cheese Salad

Mixed Fruit and Vegetable Salad

81

MIXED FRUIT AND VEGETABLE SALAD

Serves 6

3 medium-size carrots

3 apples

2 pears

6 celery sticks

1 small green pepper

1 grapefruit

½ cucumber

3 oz (75 g) raisins

½ pint (300 ml) natural yogurt

lemon juice

salt and pepper

The yogurt and lemon dressing for this mixed salad unifies the fruit and vegetables and gives them a tangy freshness. This is a salad which can be a light meal in itself, served with fresh Granary bread.

Peel and grate the carrots, core and slice the apples and pears, and finely slice the celery and the pepper. Peel the grapefruit and divide it up into segments. Peel and dice the cucumber and mix all the ingredients, in the yogurt. Season with lemon juice, salt and pepper.

HERBED CHEESE SALAD

Serves 4

1 lb (450 g) cottage cheese

5 fl oz (150 ml) carton of soured cream

1 tablespoon (15 ml spoon) each chopped chives, dill and tarragon

1 cucumber, peeled and diced

1 red pepper, diced

1 tablespoon (15 ml spoon) grated onion

8 lettuce leaves

salt and pepper

mayonnaise

This lovely salad is always popular as a lunch dish: it is fresh and light, full of different flavours, and pretty to look at as well.

Combine the cottage cheese with the soured cream and chopped herbs, cucumber and pepper. Season with the grated onion, salt and pepper, and toss well. Pile on a bed of lettuce and serve with mayonnaise.

PASTA AND LENTIL SALAD

Serves 4

8 oz (225 g) pasta shapes or
4 oz (100 g) rice

8 oz (225 g) green lentils,
soaked overnight and cooked

4 celery sticks, sliced

lots of chopped parsley

olive oil

3 cloves of garlic, crushed

salt and pepper

I am extremely fond of pasta in salads, and the combination here with lentils is wholesome and satisfying. Use lots of garlic – the pasta seems to absorb it! You can also try this salad using rice instead of pasta, and add any variety of chopped vegetables to it to ring the changes.

Cook the pasta shapes 'al dente', drain, and while still warm add the lentils, sliced celery and chopped parsley. Dress liberally with olive oil and season with masses of garlic, salt and pepper. This salad is best eaten after 24 hours when all the tastes have permeated the pasta.

FRENCH RICE SALAD

Serves 4

8 oz (225 g) tomatoes

1 large red pepper, de-seeded

12 green olives, stoned

2 oz (50 g) dry-roasted
peanuts

8 oz (225 g) wild or basmati
rice, cooked

4 tablespoons (4 × 15 ml
spoon) vinaigrette dressing

2 cloves of garlic, crushed

salt and pepper

This is an excellent salad for a buffet table – it looks elegant, tastes good, and is a nourishing dish which goes well with any cold foods.

Chop the tomatoes fairly finely and cut the pepper into short thin strips. Halve the olives, chop the peanuts coarsely and add all these to the rice. Toss in the vinaigrette and season to taste with salt, pepper and garlic. Leave to marinate for an hour or so.

CUCUMBER WITH ORANGES AND SOURED CREAM

½ pint (300 ml) soured cream

1 tablespoon (15 ml spoon) chopped mint

1 teaspoon (5 ml spoon) sugar

1 clove of garlic, crushed

3 oranges

1 cucumber

1 lettuce

2 large heads of chicory

salt and pepper

To garnish:

finely chopped chives

A summery salad this, light and refreshing, and an excellent accompaniment to quiches or vol-au-vents, or with other salads on a party table.

Mix the soured cream with the finely chopped mint, salt, pepper, sugar and garlic to taste. Peel, seed and segment the oranges, and peel and dice the cucumber. Shred the lettuce and cut the chicory into thin rounds. Toss all in the soured cream dressing and chill throughly. Sprinkle with chopped chives before serving.

Spinach and Mushroom Salad
Cucumber with Oranges and Soured Cream
French Rice Salad
Red Kidney Beans with Walnuts

RED KIDNEY BEANS WITH WALNUTS

Serves 4

8 oz (225 g) can of red
kidney beans, drained

1 small fennel root, sliced
and chopped finely

1 small onion, chopped
finely

4 oz (100 g) shelled
walnuts, chopped coarsely

a small bunch of parsley,
chopped finely

4 tablespoons (4 × 15 ml
spoon) olive oil

3 cloves of garlic, crushed

salt and pepper

*A rich and nourishing salad this, one for a robust
appetite. Its colours are as strong as its taste – the deep
maroon, dark green and white of kidney beans, fennel
and garlic.*

Mix the kidney beans with the fennel, onion,
walnuts and parsley. Season the olive oil with
lots of garlic, salt, and pepper and dress the
vegetable mixture with it. Allow to marinate for
an hour or two before serving.

SPINACH AND MUSHROOM SALAD

Serves 4

¾ lb (350 g) young spinach
leaves

6 oz (175 g) button
mushrooms

2 tablespoons (2 × 15 ml
spoon) olive oil

juice of ½ lemon

3 tablespoons (3 × 15 ml
spoon) soured cream

salt and pepper

*The taste of raw spinach is an acquired one, but once
acquired, it is delicious with fresh button mushrooms
and a sharp, creamy dressing. This salad goes
especially well with egg dishes – omelettes, soufflés
and the Gougère on page 56. It is also good as a starter
in its own right.*

Wash, dry and shred the spinach leaves and
arrange in a large, flat salad bowl. Slice the
mushrooms ¼ inch (5 mm) thick and place in
the centre. Mix the oil, lemon juice and soured
cream, and season to taste with salt and pepper.
Dribble in a lattice pattern all over the spinach
leaves and mushrooms and serve.

CARROT PUFFS

2 oz (50 g) butter

7 fl oz (200 ml) water

2 oz (50 g) flour

2 eggs

1 lb (450 g) carrots, boiled for 20 minutes

salt and pepper

These golden puffs, crisp on the outside and creamy inside, are stunning – quite one of the best ways of transforming the humble carrot. They are a great success with all age-groups, and wonderful food for the family.

Put the butter and water together in a pan and bring to the boil. Stir in the flour and keep stirring over a gentle heat until the mixture is well-amalgamated. Then, off the heat, stir in the eggs one at a time until they are completely absorbed and the mixture is shiny. Purée the carrots in the liquidiser and add to the mixture. Season to taste.

Deep-fry tablespoonsful of the mixture in very hot oil until they are puffed and golden on both sides. Drain on kitchen paper towelling and keep hot. Serve as soon as possible.

SEPTEMBER SALAD

Serves 6

1 crispy lettuce

1 large green pepper, lightly grilled

1 lb (450 g) marrow, peeled, cooked and diced

4 oz (100 g) green lentils, cooked

vinaigrette dressing

1 clove of garlic, crushed

curry paste

4 oz (100 g) dry-roasted peanuts, chopped coarsely

salt and pepper

I call this September Salad because I first made it in the early autumn during the usual marrow glut. I was surprised at how very tasty cold marrow is, and with the green pepper to give a strong taste and nuts to give the crunch, this is a beautiful dish.

Shred the lettuce and slice the pepper, discarding the seeds, stalk and pith. Add to the marrow and lentils in a salad bowl, and dress with the vinaigrette seasoned to taste with salt, pepper, garlic, and a touch of curry paste. Just before serving toss in the chopped peanuts.

JERUSALEM ARTICHOKE SALAD

Serves 4

1 lb (450 g) jerusalem
artichokes, cooked and
peeled

1 large head of chicory

1 small red pepper

6 tablespoons (6 × 15 ml
spoon) vinaigrette dressing

salt and pepper

*I am a devotee of jerusalem artichokes: I think that
their taste is outstanding, as delicate and distinctive as
asparagus, and far cheaper! The addition of chicory
adds a crunchiness to this salad, the red pepper, a touch
of colour.*

Slice the artichokes into ¼-inch (5 mm) slices,
and cut the chicory into thin rounds. Shred the
pepper and remove the stalk, seeds and pith.
Mix all together in the vinaigrette and season to
taste with salt and pepper.

PARSLEYED POTATO SALAD

Serves 4

1½ lb (675 g) new potatoes

2 large gherkins

4 oz (100 g) chopped
parsley

4 tablespoons (4 × 15 ml
spoon) mayonnaise

2 tablespoons (2 × 15 ml
spoon) single cream

1 oz (25 g) chopped walnuts

*Use waxy new potatoes for this salad, and masses of
parsley – you will find that it is a far cry from the
undistinguished and institutional potato salad! This
one has delicate flavours and textures that go
beautifully with cold meats.*

Cook the new potatoes in their skins and cut
them into thick slices. Slice the gherkins. Chop
the parsley extremely finely and mix all these
ingredients together with the mayonnaise and
cream. Sprinkle the walnuts over the top and
serve.

*Cauliflower, Egg and Watercress Salad
Avocado with Baby Turnip
Jerusalem Artichoke Salad
Parsleyed Potato Salad*

AVOCADO WITH BABY TURNIP

Serves 3–4

1 large, ripe avocado

4 tiny baby turnips

4 tablespoons (4 × 15 ml spoon) vinaigrette dressing

1 lettuce heart

I have to confess to a prejudice against turnips as a cooked vegetable. But when I first had this salad I was converted to raw baby ones — thinly sliced, they are deliciously spicy and crunchy, and an excellent foil here for the bland avocado.

Peel and dice the avocado. Peel and slice the turnips very thinly, and then cut the slices into thin strips. Toss with the avocado in the vinaigrette and place on a bed of lettuce leaves.

CAULIFLOWER, EGG AND WATERCRESS SALAD

Serves 4

1 small cauliflower

3 eggs

6 tablespoons (6 × 15 ml spoon) vinaigrette dressing

2 bunches of watercress

This is a pleasant salad which goes very well with cold mousses, or the Oeufs en Gelée on page 12. It also makes a light and tasty starter.

Trim the cauliflower and break it into florets. Parboil them for 4 minutes so that they are cooked but still crisp. Hard-boil the eggs, cool, and when cold cut into segments. Toss in the vinaigrette with the cauliflower and pile on to a bed of watercress.

MUSHROOM AND SULTANA SALAD

Serves 4

4 shallots

5 fl oz (150 ml) carton of natural yogurt

1 tablespoon (15 ml spoon) cider vinegar

4 oz (100 g) sultanas

8 oz (225 g) button mushrooms

salt and lots of black pepper

To garnish:

finely chopped mint

This very unusual salad is a delightful party dish, perhaps as part of a large buffet table. The textures and tastes are mouth-watering.

Chop the shallots finely and mix with the yogurt. Season with salt and lots of black pepper and the cider vinegar. Add the sultanas and allow to plump for several hours. Just before serving, toss in the thinly sliced mushrooms and sprinkle the salad with chopped mint.

BAKED CAULIFLOWER MOULD

Serves 6

2 oz (50 g) breadcrumbs

1 pint (600 ml) milk

1 oz (25 g) butter

3 oz (75 g) Cheddar cheese, grated

4 eggs, separated

1 large cauliflower, cut into tiny florets

salt and pepper

Oven temperature:
Gas Mark 3/325°F/170°C

Each time I have made this for friends they have raved about it. It makes a superb supper dish filled with the Noodles with Mushroooms on page 58, and is also spectacular as a side vegetable dish.

Soak the breadcrumbs in the heated milk. Add the butter and the cheese and season to taste with salt and pepper. Stir in the yolks and the cauliflower florets and season to taste. Beat the egg whites until very stiff and fold in. Put into a well-greased ring-mould and bake for 45 minutes or until firm. Leave to settle for at least 10 minutes before turning out on to a warm plate.

LENTILS PROVENÇALE

6 oz (150 g) green lentils, soaked overnight

1 tablespoon (15 ml spoon) mixed dried herbs

2 bay leaves

6 spring onions, sliced

8 oz (225 g) can of tomatoes, chopped

2 cloves of garlic, crushed

2 oz (50 g) black olives, stoned and chopped

1 tablespoon (15 ml spoon) capers

2 tablespoons (2 × 15 ml spoon) parmesan cheese

salt

A pungent and powerful series of tastes here, for which green lentils make an excellent base. It is hearty, country food, delicious served as a side vegetable or, with rice and fresh bread, as a main meal.

Drain the soaked lentils, cover with cold water and simmer gently for 20 minutes with the herbs and bay leaves. Add the spring onions and cook for a further 5 minutes. Drain, then add the tomatoes, garlic, olives and capers and heat through, mixing well. Season to taste with salt and leave to stand for 5–10 minutes before serving. Sprinkle the parmesan cheese over the top before dishing up

MEAL PLANNER

LUNCHES

1. Pumpkin Soup with fresh bread   16

Vegetable Salad with Tarragon Mayonnaise 70

2. Broccoli and Cheese Soup   18

Corn Rolls   76

green salad

3. Stuffed Marrow   32

Mashed Potato Special 74

green salad

4. Corn Curry   34

Mung Beans with Rice 79

Cucumber Salad with Oranges and Soured Cream   84

5. Lentil Loaf   22

Dhal   69

Stuffed Courgettes   21

6. Meatless Shepherd's Pie   22

Red Cabbage with Apples   78

Sweet and Sour Baby Onions   72

7. Aubergines with Pasta and Cheese   52

Cauliflower, Egg and Watercress Salad   90

8. Asparagus and Mushroom Flan   43

Lettuce with Cream   71

new potatoes

9. Egg and Spinach Pie 40

Pommes Dauphine   76

mixed salad

10. Ratatouille Pancakes 38

Spinach and Mushroom Salad   86

11. Spinach and Onion Pancakes   39

Deep-fried Cabbage 70

tomato salad

12. Onion Omelette 51

September Salad   87

fresh bread

13. Egg and Lettuce Gratin   66

Mixed Fruit and Vegetable Salad   82

new potatoes

14. Eggs with Peppers 64

French Rice Salad   83

green salad

15. Stuffed Tomatoes with Spinach and Cheese   19

Egg Flan with Jerusalem Artichokes   46

Baked Cauliflower Mould   91

mixed salad

16. Peppers stuffed with Sweetcorn   20

Noodles and Cheese Omelette   62

Lentils Provençale   92

Carrot Puffs   87

mixed salad

SUPPERS

1. Eggs with Mushroom Sauce   14

Stuffed Peppers   35

Parsleyed Potato Salad 88

tomato salad

2. Asparagus Squares 14

Vegetable Curry   28

Fried Rice Memsahib 68

papadoms

cucumber salad

3. Thick Pea Soup   15

Stuffed Cabbage   23

Cheese Croquettes   59

green salad

4. Chunky Courgette Soup   16

Stilton Tart   47

Jerusalem Artichoke Salad   88

mixed salad

5. Corn Pancakes   43

Tarte au Moutarde   40

Roasted Peppers Vinaigrette   75

coleslaw

6. Asparagus Vol-au-vents   44

Tomato Soufflé   63

Pasta with Aubergine
 Sauce   66

green salad

7. Poached Eggs en
  Choux   55

Tagliatelle with Herb
 Sauce   60

mixed salad

8. Red Kidney Beans
  with Walnuts   86

Cannelloni with
 Mushrooms and Basil
 54

green salad

9. Baby Pizzas   27

Vegetable Risotto   35

Baked Chicory   74

Herbed Cheese Salad
 82

DINNER
PARTIES

1. Aubergine Purée   11

Oeufs en Gelée   12

Vegetable Kebabs   32

Dhal   69

Fried Rice Memsahib
 68

2. Olivade   10

Leeks à la Grecque   12

Gougère   56

Vegetable Salad with
 Tarragon Mayonnaise
 70

new potatoes and
 broccoli

3. Mung Crunch   8

Avocado and Spinach
 Soup   15

Leek Purée Vol-au-
 vent   44

Gianfranco's Pasta Salad
 58

Roasted Peppers
 Vinaigrette   75

green salad

4. Cheese Wafers   8

Cold Cucumber Soup
 18

Stuffed Mushrooms
 23

Lettuce with Cream   71

Runner Beans with
 Almonds   72

Avocado with Baby
 Turnip   90

green salad

5. Little Tomato Pies
 10

Spicy Vegetable
 Casserole   26

Fried Rice Memsahib
 68

papadoms

green salad

6. Green Pea Chowder
 19

Vegetable Spring Rolls
 30

Spicy Noodles   63

Vegetable Gratin with
 Cucumber   71

green salad

7. Fettuccine with Garlic
 and Coriander   62

Carrot Soufflé with
 Ginger   31

Chinese Stir-fry
 Vegetables   80

green salad

INDEX TO RECIPES

Design and layout: Ken Vail Graphic Design
Photography: Laurie Evans
Food preparation for photography: Anne Ager
Stylist: Lesley Richardson
Typesetting: Westholme Graphics Ltd
Printed and bound by Balding & Mansell Limited
Wisbech, Cambs